T0114109

Cambridge Elements ≡

Elements in Experimental Political Science
edited by
James N. Druckman
Northwestern University

ABSTRACTION IN EXPERIMENTAL DESIGN: TESTING THE TRADEOFFS

Ryan Brutger
University of California–Berkeley

Joshua D. Kertzer
Harvard University

Jonathan Renshon
University of Wisconsin–Madison

Chagai M. Weiss
University of Wisconsin–Madison

CAMBRIDGE
UNIVERSITY PRESS

CAMBRIDGE
UNIVERSITY PRESS

University Printing House, Cambridge CB2 8BS, United Kingdom

One Liberty Plaza, 20th Floor, New York, NY 10006, USA

477 Williamstown Road, Port Melbourne, VIC 3207, Australia

314–321, 3rd Floor, Plot 3, Splendor Forum, Jasola District Centre,
New Delhi – 110025, India

103 Penang Road, #05–06/07, Visioncrest Commercial, Singapore 238467

Cambridge University Press is part of the University of Cambridge.

It furthers the University's mission by disseminating knowledge in the pursuit of
education, learning, and research at the highest international levels of excellence.

www.cambridge.org
Information on this title: www.cambridge.org/9781108995597
DOI: 10.1017/9781108999533

© Ryan Brutger, Joshua D. Kertzer, Jonathan Renshon, and Chagai M. Weiss 2022

First published 2022

A catalogue record for this publication is available from the British Library.

ISBN 978-1-108-99559-7 Paperback
ISSN 2633-3368 (online)
ISSN 2633-335X (print)

Additional resources for this publication at
https://www.cambridge.org/abstraction-appendix

Abstraction in Experimental Design: Testing the Tradeoffs

Elements in Experimental Political Science

DOI: 10.1017/9781108999533
First published online: September 2022

Ryan Brutger
University of California-Berkeley

Joshua D. Kertzer
Harvard University

Jonathan Renshon
University of Wisconsin–Madison

Chagai M. Weiss
University of Wisconsin–Madison

Author for correspondence: Ryan Brutger, brutger@berkeley.edu

Abstract: Political scientists designing experiments often face the question of how abstract or detailed their experimental stimuli should be. Typically, this question is framed in terms of tradeoffs relating to experimental control and generalizability: the more context introduced into studies, the less control, and the more difficulty generalizing the results. Yet, we have reason to question this tradeoff, and there is relatively little systematic evidence to rely on when calibrating the degree of abstraction in studies. We make two contributions. First, we provide a theoretical framework that identifies and considers the consequences of three dimensions of abstraction in experimental design: situational hypotheticality, actor identity, and contextual detail. Second, we field a range of survey experiments, varying these levels of abstraction. We find that situational hypotheticality does not substantively change experimental results, but increased contextual detail dampens treatment effects and the salience of actor identities moderates results in specific situations.

Keywords: experiments, abstract, abstraction, generalizability, survey experiments

ISBNs: 9781108995597 (PB), 9781108999533 (OC)
ISSNs: 2633-3368 (online), 2633-335X (print)

Contents

1 Introduction

Experimentalists in political science often face a question about how abstract or concrete their experimental stimuli ought to be. Should they use real country (or candidate) names and include rich detail that greatly expands the length of their vignettes, or should they avoid the use of real names and embed their treatments in stark, abstract vignettes that highlight only the most necessary components of the experiment? Should they introduce their scenarios by describing them as hypothetical, or perhaps use deception and describe them as "real?" What, if any, are the consequences to these choices and should experimentalists weigh their options differently depending on what their goals are in a given study?

These types of questions are often thought of in terms of tradeoffs relating to experimental control and generalizability. At one end of the continuum, researchers in the economics tradition tend to prefer highly stylized experiments that are deliberately light on context, even though this comes at the expense of ecological validity and mundane realism, the latter term referring to whether the study resembles, in superficial appearance, what respondents would experience in the real world (Morton and Williams, 2010, 313–14). This tradition is particularly popular in behavioral experiments in political science seeking to test the predictions of formal models (e.g., Dickson, 2009; Dawes, Loewen, and Fowler, 2011; Tingley and Walter, 2011a, b; Kanthak and Woon, 2015; Kertzer and Rathbun, 2015; LeVeck and Narang, 2017; Quek, 2017; Hundley, 2020), but also arises in survey experimental work in political science as well (e.g., Renshon, 2015; Mutz and Kim, 2017; Tingley, 2017). This approach to experiments has a storied pedigree, and can be traced back to Nobel Prize laureate Vernon Smith's (1976, 278) admonition to not "embellish the instructions with well-intentioned attempts at 'realism.'"

At the other end of the continuum, a different tradition originating in psychology has encouraged the use of rich and detailed vignette-based experiments. This approach, too, has found a foothold in political science (e.g., Rousseau and Garcia-Retamero, 2007; Brooks and Valentino, 2011; Druckman, Peterson, and Slothuus, 2013; Teele, Kalla, and Rosenbluth, 2018; Reeves and Rogowski, 2018; Bracic and Murdie, 2020; Tomz, Weeks, and Yarhi-Milo, 2020). Context-rich and detailed stimuli are in some ways a response to what has been described as the "major problem in public opinion and survey research": the "ambiguity that often arises when survey respondents are asked to make decisions and judgments from rather abstract and limited information" (Alexander and Becker, 1978, 103). The ability to generalize experimental findings to other contexts, and the degree to which an experiment triggers the psychological process that would occur in the "real world," are both thought to rise in proportion to the level of "realism" in a given vignette (Aguinis and Bradley, 2014, 361). Similarly, others argue that "concrete, realistic context" results in more "reliable assessments" of the dependent variables we care about (Steiner, Atzmüller, and Su, 2016, 53).

Political scientists seeking to navigate these tradeoffs are usually exposed to one or the other of these schools of thought regarding experimental design, and how they navigate these tradeoffs may have more to do with institutional path dependence and methodological inclinations than verifiable data or theoretical frameworks. In fact, a survey of the state of experimental methods reveals little systematic evidence about how to choose between these competing approaches. Some scholars advise that respondents perform better in more concrete and familiar settings (Reiley, 2015), while others worry that doing so reduces experimental control (Camerer, 1997). As researchers working in this area, we have been struck by the extent to which reviewers and editors often have very strong priors about how to handle these tradeoffs in experimental design, which often directly contradict one another.

And yet, as a discipline we know relatively little about the tradeoffs inherent in abstract versus concrete experimental designs and indeed whether a focus on these particular tradeoffs is the right way to understand the issue in the first place. Certainly, increasing "color in the laboratory" *may* trigger "unknown (to the experimenter) impressions and memories of past experiences over which the experimenter has no control" (Friedman, Friedman, and Sunder, 1994), but it is not obvious why sparse experiments would fare better in this respect since respondents are more than capable of bringing along their own beliefs, impressions, and thoughts "into the lab" even when not explicitly triggered to do so. A review of the broader experimental literature suggests strong disagreement on which would be a bigger problem in terms of respondents "filling in the blanks": rich, detailed experiments (e.g., Friedman, Friedman, and Sunder, 1994) or abstract, sparse studies (e.g., Alekseev, Charness, and Gneezy, 2017). And while others have noted that there is no "general theory that would give experimentalists guidance as to when stylization" might pose problems (Dickson, 2011, 61), and that this is "ultimately, an empirical issue that would have to be thrashed out by comparing data from abstract as well as contextually rich experiments" (Friedman, Friedman, and Sunder, 1994, 53–4), there is surprisingly little systematic work that does so. This forces experimentalists in political science to rely on hunches, intuitions, and tradition rather than systematic evidence and theoretical guidance.

In this Element, we explore the consequences of abstraction and detail in experimental design and innovate both theoretically and empirically. First, we offer an overarching conceptual framework outlining three different dimensions of abstraction implicated in experimental design: *situational hypotheticality, actor identity*, and *contextual detail*. We argue that there are certain types of questions where ethical or feasibility considerations mandate at least some form of hypotheticality or abstraction, while there are others where scholars have more leeway. Yet, in those cases where scholars do have leeway, we argue that the tradeoffs between abstraction and detail in experimental design are not as stark as political scientists often claim. Our overarching goal is to give researchers a conceptual framework and empirical foundation upon which they can make informed decisions.

Second, like other recent work seeking to subject conventional wisdom about experimental design principles to empirical scrutiny (Brutger et al., Forthcoming; Mullinix et al., 2015; White et al., 2018; Coppock, 2019; Mummolo and Peterson, 2019; Kertzer, 2020; Clifford, Sheagley, and Piston, 2021), we test our theoretical framework by fielding eight survey experiments and a pretest, both extending a set of popular vignette-based survey experiments across different subfields of political science, and introducing new experiments of our own – manipulating levels of abstraction along our three theorized dimensions. Doing so, we explore how experimental results change when varying different levels of abstraction in experimental stimuli. We find that varying situational hypotheticality generally does not have a significant effect on experimental results in our studies. However, we show that adding contextual detail to experimental vignettes attenuates the size of treatment effects because respondents are less likely to be able to recall the treatment. When it comes to actor identity, the results are more nuanced. We find that using certain actors, specifically those that suffer from *treatment inconsistency*, can undermine experimental results. The salience of actors can also moderate experimental findings, particularly in cue-giver experiments where respondents are likely to have more knowledge of, and stronger priors about, salient cue-givers.

The remainder of the Element proceeds as follows. Section 2 introduces our theoretical framework, in which we conceptualize three central dimensions of abstraction in experimental design. Our first dimension, *situational hypotheticality*, concerns whether a scenario is described as hypothetical or not. Existing experiments take different approaches on this dimension, describing scenarios as hypothetical, real (oftentimes engaging in deception), or set in the future. In our discussion of situational hypotheticality, we consider different rationales for adapting varying degrees of situational hypotheticality, and discuss situations that constrain experimenters' ability to adopt real or hypothetical framings. Our second dimension, *actor identity*, involves the type of actors invoked in experimental vignettes. Experiments vary significantly on this dimension, with different studies focusing on real (Boettcher III and Cobb,

2006; Nicholson, 2012), made-up (Brooks and Valentino, 2011), or unnamed (Kertzer, Renshon, and Yarhi-Milo, 2021) countries, politicians, or citizens. In our discussion of this dimension, we describe diverging rationales for employing different actors, while emphasizing technical and ethical considerations that may constrain experimenters' choices in this domain. Our third dimension, *contextual detail*, relates to the amount and type of additional context provided in a given experiment. While some experiments provide rich background context that is either related or unrelated to the treatment (e.g., McDermott and Cowden, 2001; Valentino, Neuner, and Vandenbroek, 2018), other experiments include limited background information regarding a given scenario (e.g., Tingley and Walter, 2011a; Kanthak and Woon, 2015). In our discussion of this third dimension we differentiate between different types of contextual detail, and discuss our theoretical expectations regarding their effects.

Section 3 presents our research design and provides an overview of the experiments we employ to test the three dimensions of our conceptual framework. We field a total of eight experiments (and a pretest) covering different substantive topics in political science and manipulating different (and sometimes overlapping) aspects of our framework. Our experiments include extensions of four vignette-based survey experiments: our ELITE CUES experiment, which extends Nicholson's (2012) study of elite cues in American immigration policy debates, our NUCLEAR WEAPONS experiment, which extends Press, Sagan, and Valentino's (2013) test of the nuclear taboo in public opinion toward the use of force, our IN-GROUP FAVORITISM experiment, which extends Mutz and Kim's (2017) exploration of the role of in-group favoritism in trade preferences, and two different extensions of Tomz and Weeks' (2013) DEMOCRATIC PEACE experiment. We supplement these experiments with three original studies relating to hypotheticality, actor identity, and framed around highly salient real-world events. Our VICE PRESIDENT experiment explores the dynamics of American public opinion about Joe Biden's selection of a vice-presidential candidate (fielded before the then-Democratic presidential candidate had chosen Kamala Harris as his running mate), the PROTEST experiment explores how Americans think about domestic protests (fielded as Black Lives Matter protests swept across the United States in the aftermath of the murder of George Floyd), and our WORLD HEALTH ORGANIZATION (WHO) experiment explores attitudes toward US involvement in the WHO (fielded as the Trump administration considered pulling out of the international organization in the midst of the global pandemic). The experiments we employ in this Element thus span multiple subfields of political science, and include a mix of extensions of classic studies, along with a set of original studies relating to real-world events from the news.

Section 4 discusses and tests the effects of situational hypotheticality, using each of the previously introduced experiments. We test whether respondents have adverse reactions to being told that they are assessing hypothetical scenarios by varying whether experiments are described as real, prospective, explicitly hypothetical, or left as ambiguously hypothetical, and whether the treatment itself invokes an expert's projections. The findings in this section show that varying degrees of situational hypotheticality does not generally affect the results of experiments, giving researchers significant freedom to choose how to design their vignettes. This is particularly helpful given institutional review boards' concerns about deceiving respondents. We show that experimentalists will not degrade the efficacy of their designs by labeling their vignettes as explicitly hypothetical.

Section 5 presents and interprets the results from tests considering how the choice of actor identities moderate experimental outcomes. We use the DEMOCRATIC PEACE and NUCLEAR WEAPONS studies, along with an additional pre-test, to examine how schema and treatment inconsistency alter respondent reactions. We also test how real versus fake politicians, and the salience of those politicians, alter respondents' reactions using the ELITE CUES study. Our results show that treatment inconsistency poses a large problem for experimentalists – larger than schema inconsistency – because respondents do not find the treatment credible. We also find that our ELITE CUES study yields larger effects when using real-world salient actors. In light of these findings we prescribe two recommendations: First, experimenters must ensure that their actors are treatment-consistent. Second, if employing real actors, experimenters should introduce scope conditions to contextualize the size of their effects.

Section 6 analyzes the effects of contextual detail using the NUCLEAR WEAPONS and IN-GROUP FAVORITISM experiments. These studies vary both the amount of context provided and the substance of the content – whether it is "filler" or "charged." We find that increasing context reduces average treatment effect sizes. Further, we show that these attenuated effects can be linked to respondents' decreased treatment recall when presented with lengthier vignettes. Importantly, however, adding or subtracting content in vignettes does not alter the core results of a given study. Therefore, building on our findings, we elaborate on the conditions in which a researcher may prefer to choose a sparse vignette versus a contextually rich experimental design.

Section 7 moves beyond an analysis of average treatment effects to consider how dimensions of abstraction manifest across different types of respondents. There are reasons to believe that individual-level factors may influence the effects of abstraction by shaping how respondents view the actors or interpret the vignette. Thus, we evaluate how political knowledge, need for cognition,

strength of partisanship, and affect toward countries interact with the various
dimensions of abstraction. This analysis tests the microfoundations of our theory and helps inform the design choices of researchers who are interested in
particular subject pools.

   In Section 8 we tie together the main findings with a set of conclusions and
recommendations. We emphasize that there are many times when experimentalists have significant degrees of freedom to design their experiments as they
see fit, with relatively few tradeoffs. However, we also highlight the situations
where design choices are highly consequential, such as choosing a treatment-
inconsistent actor, or potential power concerns that may result from the more
conservative treatment effects when using context-rich vignettes.

2 Conceptual Framework: Dimensions of Abstraction in Experimental Design

One of the many design choices political scientists face when using experimental methods concerns the appropriate level of *abstraction*. There is a rich
literature on abstraction in philosophy, psychology, and cognitive science,
which often operationalizes abstraction in slightly different ways (e.g., Cantor and Mischel, 1979; Semin and Fiedler, 1988; Paivio, 1990; Colburn and
Shute, 2007). For our purposes, we borrow from construal level theory in social
psychology in defining abstraction as a higher-level representation (Sartori,
1970, 1040–46; Trope and Liberman, 2003). It involves making "a distinction
between primary, defining features, which are relatively stable and invariant,
and secondary features, which may change with changes in context and hence
are omitted from the higher-level representation" (Shapira et al., 2012, 231).
As Table 1 shows, an abstract representation is sparse and decontextualized,
reduced to the object's most central elements (e.g., "a military invasion"),
whereas a concrete representation is contextualized and rich in specific detail,
including subordinate considerations (e.g., "Russia sending military forces into
eastern Ukraine").

   Two points here are relevant for our purposes. First, in specifying which elements of a construct are primary and which are secondary, the act of abstraction
is inherently a theoretical phenomenon, rather than an empirical one. In fact,
this is exactly why discussions of abstraction in design that center on experimental control and generalizability are incomplete without consideration of
construct validity: whether our operationalizations "meaningfully capture the
ideas contained in the concepts" (Collier and Adcock, 2001, 529). Construct
validity is relevant here in a number of ways. McDermott (2002) points out that
threats to construct validity come from manipulations that affect other concepts

Table 1 Conceptualizing abstraction

Abstract	Concrete
High level of construal	Low level of construal
Decontextualized	Contextualized
Primary features	Secondary features
Sparse	Complex
Superordinate elements	Subordinate elements

Source: Trope and Liberman (2003, 405).

simultaneously, exactly the concern that experimentalists have tended to frame as being about experimental control; thus manipulations that trigger multiple things at once affect both control *and* construct validity. Similarly, Findley, Kikuta, and Denly (2021, 371) note that "an externally valid treatment variable must have construct validity."

Second, questions about the appropriate level of abstraction loom large in a variety of issues in experimental design: whether experiments should be "stylized" or "contextually rich" (Dickson, 2011; Kreps and Roblin, 2019), use real or hypothetical actors (McDonald, 2020; Nielson, Hyde, and Kelley, 2019), and refer to imminent, future, or hypothetical situations. In this sense, experiments can be abstract or concrete along multiple dimensions at the same time. In this section, we suggest that abstraction in experimental design can be conceptualized along at least three dimensions, and that it is more fruitful to disentangle different types of abstraction in experimental design rather than presume that questions of abstraction can be neatly collapsed into tradeoffs between experimental control and generalizability.

The discussion begins by presenting the three dimensions of abstraction in experimental design we focus on here: situational hypotheticality, actor identity, and contextual detail.[1] We classify a set of recent experiments in political science along these dimensions in Table 2, and then review each dimension in detail.[2] We then show that tradeoffs between experimental control and generalizability are not always so clean.

---

[1] This typology is, of course, not exhaustive, and we encourage future work to incorporate other dimensions as well.

[2] Although our interest in this Element is in abstraction in experimental methods, similar questions about abstraction also arise in formal modeling, and in quantitative and qualitative methods alike (Clarke and Primo, 2012).

Table 2 Abstraction in experimental political science

Type of experiment	Example	Type of abstraction		
		Situational hypotheticality	Actor identity	Contextual detail
Audit experiment	Butler and Broockman (2011)	Deception	N/A	Med
Conjoint experiment	Hainmueller and Hopkins (2015)	Ambiguous	Unnamed	Med
Economics-style lab experiment	Kanthak and Woon (2015)	Real	Unnamed	Low
Endorsement experiment	Lyall, Blair, and Imai (2013)	Real	Real	Med
Framing experiment	Nelson, Clawson, and Oxley (1997)	Deception	Real	High
Lab-in-the-field experiment	Habyarimana et al. (2007)	Real	Unnamed	Low
Vignette-based experiment	Tomz (2007)	Ambiguous	Unnamed	Med
War game	McDermott et al. (2007)	Simulation	Artificial	Med
Field experiment	Lyall, Zhou, and Imai (2020)	Real	Real	High

2.1 Situational Hypotheticality

The first dimension of abstraction in experimental design concerns whether a scenario is described as hypothetical or not.[3] The rationale for using hypothetical scenarios in survey experiments is simple: in their most stylized form, experimentalists make causal inferences by drawing comparisons between two different states of the world, randomly assigning participants to either a treatment condition, or control. Some experiments intervene by giving respondents in the treatment condition information about the world that they might not otherwise have (e.g., Butler, Nickerson et al., 2011; Raffler, 2019), but especially in survey experiments, experimentalists often manipulate features of the world itself. In order to manipulate features of the world in this manner, experimentalists must either engage in deception, showing respondents mock news articles purported to be real (e.g., Brader, Valentino, and Suhay, 2008; Arceneaux, 2012), or find another way to justify – whether to respondents, or to IRBs – why the scenario being described to respondents deviates from the one they are in.

There are a variety of techniques experimentalists often employ. One is to explicitly describe the scenario as hypothetical: respondents in Boettcher's study (2004, 344), for example, are asked to "envision a hypothetical presidency apart from the current administration." Others implicitly or ambiguously invoke hypotheticality: respondents participating in conjoint experiments studying immigration preferences, for example (e.g., Hainmueller and Hopkins, 2015), are presumably not under the illusion that the immigrants they are being asked to choose between are real. Another widely used form of ambiguous hypotheticality is to describe a scenario as set in the future, as in Mattes and Weeks (2019), who for example, tell respondents, "We are going to describe a situation the United States could face in the future, in 2027."

The rationales for these design choices are often not explicitly stated, but usually involves concerns that respondents will not take studies as seriously when scenarios are presented as explicitly hypothetical – the sense that researchers asking hypothetical questions will be rewarded with hypothetical answers (Converse and Presser, 1986, 23), or induce respondents to engage in different forms of information processing than they would in the real world (Mutz, 2021). Similar concerns have been raised by psychologists, who have found that the use of hypothetical versus real scenarios has important implications

---

[3] Note that the relevant question here is whether the scenario is *presented* as hypothetical, rather than whether the details described in the scenario are in fact hypothetical; as we note here and in Section 4, experiments utilizing deception, for example, may present hypothetical scenarios as if they are real.

for respondents' behavior, and may affect how they evaluate moral considerations, for example (FeldmanHall et al., 2012; Bostyn, Sevenhant, and Roets, 2018). Experimentalists operating out of an economics-style tradition tend to avoid both deception and situational hypotheticality in order to accentuate the effects of incentives (Morton and Williams, 2010). Yet, there is relatively little empirical work investigating the conditions in which situational hypotheticality affects responses in the contexts of political science experiments and theories.

2.2 Actor Identity

The second dimension of abstraction involves the identity of the actors invoked in experimental vignettes: are they real, or artificial? Some experimenters explicitly use real-world actors in contexts ripped from the headlines, as in Boettcher III and Cobb's (2006) study of how casualty frames shape support for the war in Iraq, or in Evers, Fisher, and Schaaf (2019), which experimentally investigates audience costs using Donald Trump and Barack Obama. In this sense, the artificiality of the actors in an experiment is distinct from the hypotheticality of the situations in which actors are embedded. Indeed, experimenters often use real-world actors in hypothetical scenarios. For example, Kriner and Shen's (2014) casualty sensitivity experiments explore how many casualties Americans would be willing to bear in a series of "hypothetical" interventions in "real" countries (Somalia, Darfur, Iran, and Liberia). In this case, the military interventions are artificial and prospective, while the relevant target countries are real.

Moving up the ladder of abstraction, some experimenters describe hypothetical scenarios in artificial countries, in order to exert complete control over how much information participants bring to bear. For example, Brooks and Valentino (2011) describe a conflict between "Malaguay and Westria," and Rubenzer and Redd (2010) describe a crisis in the state of "Gorendy." Taking this approach a step forward, many experimentalists use unnamed countries, describing target states as "Country A" or "Country B" (Johns and Davies, 2012; Yarhi-Milo, Kertzer, and Renshon, 2018), or simply referring to "a country" rather than providing a label (Tomz and Weeks, 2013).[4]

Concerns about actor identity and hypotheticality are not limited to the subfield of international relations. In comparative politics, Banerjee and colleagues (2014) describe hypothetical representatives (running for office in hypothetical districts) to study the concerns of voters in rural India. "Hypothetical candidate"

---

[4] In instructions to participants, researchers often note that this generality is "for scientific validity."

experiments are also a long-running feature in the study of American politics (as in Rosenwasser et al., 1987; Colleau et al., 1990; Kam and Zechmeister, 2013) – and are particularly common in conjoint experiments – although the results here are mixed. In a meta-analysis of 111 studies of negative campaigning, Lau, Sigelman, and Rovner (2007) find that experiments featuring hypothetical candidates do not offer significantly different results from those featuring real ones. McDonald (2020), in contrast, argues that experiments on hypothetical candidates increase cognitive burden and produce larger treatment effects than experiments on candidates about which respondents have strong priors.

As with the case of situational hypotheticality, the logic of using unnamed or hypothetical actors stems directly from the questions being tested. Political scientists turned to experimental methods to study the effects of candidate gender (Huddy and Terkildsen, 1993; Sanbonmatsu, 2002; Brooks and Valentino, 2011), for example, precisely because it is difficult to find two real-world candidates identical to one another on all dimensions other than their gender. The same is true in studies of race in politics (Burge, Wamble, and Cuomo, 2020; Wamble, 2020), or ethnicity (Dunning and Harrison, 2010, though see Adida, 2015). In an international relations (IR) context, it is hard to think of two real-world countries that are identical in all respects but one, meaning that IR scholars interested in manipulating the effects of regime type, military capabilities, or foreign policy interests usually do so with fictional or hypothetical countries (e.g., Rousseau and Garcia-Retamero, 2007).

2.3 Contextual Detail

The third dimension of abstraction involves the amount of additional context provided in an experiment. Traditionally, questions about contextual detail in experimental research were largely a function of the experimental medium itself: survey experiments conducted by telephone, for example, required relatively short vignettes so that respondents would be able to process the necessary details (e.g., Herrmann, Tetlock, and Visser, 1999), whereas psychology-style experiments taking place in the lab could present respondents with much richer stimuli (e.g., Druckman, 2003). The rise of online survey experiments, however, has given researchers a much wider range of options.

Press, Sagan, and Valentino (2013) present a lengthy newspaper article that provides participants with a large amount of context, as do experiments in American politics that generate fake campaign advertisements or news clips (Brader, Valentino, and Suhay, 2008). In contrast, other experiments present relatively little information. Trager and Vavreck (2011), for example, manipulate the president's strategy in a foreign policy crisis as well as information about the US domestic political environment, but as with most audience cost experiments, they say relatively little about the context of the intervention itself. Most experiments in the experimental economics tradition offer relatively little contextual detail at all, deliberately paring the design down to be void of explicit political content (e.g., Tingley and Walter, 2011b; Kanthak and Woon, 2015; Quek, 2017).

The argument usually offered in favor of contextual detail is that it increases realism and respondent engagement. Anecdotally, in some of our own research, when we include open-ended prompts at the ends of survey experiments soliciting feedback from participants, one of the most frequent comments we have received involved scenarios being "too vague": participants wanted more information in order to help them make up their minds. Yet, apart from Kreps and Roblin (2019) and Bansak and colleagues (2021), there has been little empirical work to adjudicate what the consequences of providing richer or sparser stimuli might be. Bansak and colleagues (2021) use a clever multi-stage conjoint design to first find "filler attributes" (information uncorrelated with the object of interest in the study) and then experimentally vary the amount of filler in the second stage, finding relatively stable treatment effects even with large numbers (up to thirty-five) of filler items. Kreps and Roblin (2019) focus on treatment "formats," in particular the difference between information presented in mock news stories versus short/long vignettes (with a slight conflation of the "length" versus "format" dimensions), finding that respondent attention (as a measure of satisficing) was unaffected by the presentational format.

This discussion suggests that what is often referred to as "contextual detail" is actually composed of at least three related dimensions. The first is simply the volume of information provided: more or less information can be provided in an experiment to supplement the treatments and add "realism." We might, for example, provide a long or short biography of a candidate or background to an international dispute. The second concerns *how* the information is presented, and here there have been examples of any number of treatment formats in experiments, from bullet-pointed vignettes (Tomz, 2007), to mock news stories (Druckman and Nelson, 2003) and "ad-watch" style reports (Valentino, Neuner, and Vandenbroek, 2018). The third is the content of the information itself, which is orthogonal to its volume. Any bit of information may be classified as either what Bansak and colleagues (2021) call "filler" or its opposite, what we term "charged" content, which may interact with the treatment in some way and affect the results of a study through a mechanism other than simple respondent satisficing. If a president's "favorite highway" is filler, then Bansak et al. (2021) also show that other attributes (e.g., previous occupation and number of children) can be associated with the object of interest and are thus ill-suited to be added simply to increase the "realism" of a vignette. But while they show that satisficing is less of a problem than we might expect once we introduce filler attributes, we are still largely in the dark with respect to understanding how the addition of charged (versus filler) content affects our interpretation of experimental results.

2.4 Navigating the Tradeoffs

In sum, although political scientists tend to recognize that tradeoffs between abstract and concrete experiments exist, there is less certainty about how one should navigate them. Often, for example, political scientists run both abstract and concrete versions of their experiment to test whether the results hold (e.g., Herrmann, Tetlock, and Visser, 1999; Levine and Palfrey, 2007; Rousseau and Garcia-Retamero, 2007; Berinsky, 2009; Horowitz and Levendusky, 2011; LeVeck et al., 2014; Landau-Wells, 2018; Renshon, Dafoe, and Huth, 2018; Nielson, Hyde, and Kelley, 2019). However, doing so can be somewhat inefficient, as adjusting levels of abstraction on multiple dimensions simultaneously provides limited insight regarding the specific dimension driving experimental outcomes.[5]

There are some circumstances where for logistical or ethical reasons, experimenters will be constrained in terms of how abstract or concrete their stimuli will be. For example, researchers are limited in their ability to select real-world actors when studying the effects of race and gender in candidate selection, or the effects of country-level characteristics on foreign policy preferences. Additionally, there are experiments where some form of situational hypotheticality is required (often at the demand of IRBs) to avoid the use of deception, and some contexts where the use of deception raises ethical challenges: for example, telling respondents that a real-world political candidate is unethical (e.g., Butler and Powell, 2014). Experimentalists using subject pools that prohibit deception, or seeking to publish in journals that do the same (Morton and Williams, 2010), will face similar restrictions in choosing the optimal level of abstraction in experimental design.

In other cases, however, experimentalists have more of a choice when designing their studies. While political scientists often understand abstraction in experimental design in terms of tradeoffs between experimental control, on the one hand, and generalizability, on the other, we argue that the implications

---

[5] Moreover, given the presence of a budget constraint, running two versions of the same experiment to preempt questions about abstraction can also lead to statistical power problems.

of abstraction in experimental design for each principle are actually more complex. There are some instances where an increase in abstraction may enhance experimental control, and others where an increase in abstraction may come at the expense of experimental control. Since experimentalists may not exercise as much control over their respondents as we like to think, more abstract stimuli may not necessarily be more generalizable. We suggest, then, that the tradeoff between abstract and concrete experimental designs represents something of a paradox: many of the circumstances in which experimentalists have the most leeway in terms of the abstraction of design choices may in fact be the ones where the tradeoffs between different design choices are the least consequential.

Experimental Control

Experimenters seek to obtain "control" over the ways in which respondents construe the contextual features of vignettes, in order to ensure proper implementation of their experimental designs.[6] When experimental vignettes invoke different reactions among different types of respondents – or perhaps invoke reactions the researcher never intended – experimenters can risk losing control over their study, raising concerns regarding internal validity. By varying the information provided along the three aforementioned levels of abstraction, experimenters can potentially shape the degree of control they obtain.

Yet, we argue that navigating the relationship between control, generalizability, and abstraction requires further consideration. First, the relationship between abstraction and control varies based upon the dimension under investigation. Increasing contextual detail is often thought to enhance experimental control, by fixing the type and degree of information that all subjects share regarding an issue area. For example, when implementing an endorsement experiment regarding a fictional or real immigration policy (Nicholson, 2012), researchers can provide detailed information regarding: (i) who initiated the policy, (ii) when it comes into effect, and (iii) how it relates to previous policies. Presumably, this information can ensure an informational common denominator, and avoid a situation in which respondents with different background knowledge construe the experimental vignette in diverging ways.

---

6 Similarly, experimenters seek to control the construal of treatments themselves. As Tomz and Weeks (2013) point out, if participants who are told that a country is democratic are also likely to assume that democracies are more likely to win the wars they fight, the regime type treatment becomes double-barreled, manipulating omitted details (see also Kertzer and Brutger, 2016; Dafoe, Zhang, and Caughey, 2018).

In contrast, increased detail in terms of actor identity is usually argued to reduce experimental control. In an international relations context, Herrmann, Tetlock, and Visser (1999, 556) note that "the use of real countries [adds] a degree of realism … but it also sacrifice[s] a degree of experimental control. Affective reactions to the various countries may differ, and [characteristics of the countries] may not be perceived uniformly by all participants." In American politics, Reeves and Rogowski (2018, 428) write that "the use of hypothetical candidates comes at the cost of reducing the real-world attributes of the experiment, but this cost is offset by removing respondents from their feelings about any actual politician, which could serve as confounders." These examples suggest that by introducing real-world actors and adding detail into vignettes, experimenters lose control over their respondents – the opposite of conventional wisdom about the effects of contextual detail.

More generally, it may be somewhat misleading to think that by turning from real to hypothetical actors, or from contextually sparse to rich vignettes, experimenters gain control over their study. Indeed, when presented with relatively pared down stimuli, participants often "fill in the blanks." For example, scenarios in which "a country sent its military to take over a neighboring country" and in which the United States is considering sending troops to repel the invader (Herrmann, Tetlock, and Visser, 1999; Tomz, 2007; Trager and Vavreck, 2011) may lead participants to think of the Gulf War.[7] Moreover, different types of respondents may invoke different mental schema when faced with the same abstract scenario; depending on a respondent's generation, "repel an invader" experiments may invoke Korea, Vietnam, Iraq, or none of the above. Likewise, it is possible that different respondents will exhibit diverging reactions to additional contextual detail, leading experimenters to lose, rather than gain control. Adopting an abstract design can thus either increase or decrease experimental control such that the tradeoff here may not be as clean cut as experimentalists sometimes suggest.

Even if experimenters may have more leeway when choosing the appropriate level of abstraction for actor identity than is often claimed, this does not mean that all concrete actor identities are equally desirable. In particular, experimenters should attend to at least two considerations when choosing real-world actors, which we describe in detail in Section 5. The first is *schema consistency*

---

[7] Similarly, in their survey experiment on the effect of regime type on support for the use of force, Johns and Davies (2012, 1043) note that the vignette is "loosely based on recent debates about Iran but [makes] no explicit reference to that or any other real country," acknowledging the possibility that at least politically sophisticated participants are likely thinking of Iran when they answer the questions.

(Hashtroudi et al., 1984): in studies where actors are fixed across treatment arms, is the choice of actor reasonable given the scenario in which the actor is embedded? For example, in experimental scenarios in which a country is pursuing a nuclear weapons program (e.g., Tomz and Weeks, 2013), experimental control decreases if the experimenter chooses a country that already has nuclear weapons (e.g., Russia), or a country that respondents think is unlikely to pursue them (e.g., Canada). One might be concerned that if a schema-inconsistent actor is chosen, the respondent is less likely to believe the scenario or remember the treatment, thus weakening the treatment effect.

The second consideration (not mutually exclusive) is *treatment consistency*: if the treatment manipulates an attribute of an actor, are all levels of the attribute being manipulated seen as plausible by respondents? In candidate selection experiments, for example, it would be difficult to manipulate the partisanship of politicians with well-known partisan identities, or to manipulate the policy stances of politicians on issues where they have already taken prominent positions. If respondents do not perceive the treatment as consistent with the identity of the actor, then the experimenter is likely to lose control since the respondent may not comply with the treatment, attenuating the treatment effect.

Generalizability

While experimental control is a fundamental aspect in designing vignettes, scholars may very well be concerned by other factors such as generalizability – the extent to which results from a given study speak to a broader set of real-world scenarios. Like control, degrees of generalizability may be shaped by levels of abstraction in experimental design. Thus, when framing an experiment as hypothetical or real, and when selecting particular actors, and levels of contextual detail, researchers may condition the degree to which their results generalize beyond a particular context.

Oftentimes, experimenters adopt unnamed actors in experimental vignettes in order to enhance generalizability. At least implicitly, the selection of an unnamed actor is motivated by the fact that a researcher's quantity of interest is a main effect rather than a conditional effect. For example, researchers studying reputation may be interested in the effect of past behavior on forming reputations for resolve in general, not the effect of past behavior on forming reputations for resolve for Iran specifically (Renshon, Dafoe, and Huth, 2018).

Yet, it is unclear that increased abstraction actually increases generalizability. First, when we generalize from these experiments to the problems in the real world that motivate us to conduct them in the first place, selecting unnamed actors may lead us to miss important sources of treatment hetero-geneity, and may even make it harder to generalize results to any motivating real-world cases.[8] For example, because respondents are often "pre-treated" with partisan cues prior to participating in our studies (Gaines, Kuklinski, and Quirk, 2007), experimenters might deliberately choose nonpartisan scenarios where these pretreatment effects are minimized, lest the effects of partisanship swamp or overwhelm the treatments of interest. Yet, if many political phenom-ena have a partisan hue, the absence of partisan dynamics in the experiment actually makes it harder to generalize these results (McDonald, 2020).

Similarly, the degree of contextual detail provided by experimenters might shape the extent that findings from an experiment can generalize to real-world scenarios. If participants in experiments only receive two pieces of information, one of which is the treatment being randomly assigned, the rel-ative "dosage" of the treatment is likely to be unrealistically high, and may not hold in a more naturalistic setting (Barabas and Jerit, 2010). In contrast, if the treatment is presented to participants embedded in a larger amount of information (a full newspaper article, rather than just a few bullet points, for example), the treatment is likely to exert a (realistically) smaller effect. The same consideration holds with situational hypotheticality: rather than bolster generalizability, it may in fact decrease it, if when given strictly hypotheti-cal scenarios, respondents provide strictly hypothetical answers (Converse and Presser, 1986).

In sum, then, although experimentalists frequently think about experimental control and generalizability as two competing priorities, the latter linked to abstract designs, and the former to concrete ones, it is not clear that such a view is appropriate. Adding contextual detail can increase control, but choosing real-world actors may lower it. Respondents given pared down stimuli can still "fill in the blanks," such that more abstract designs are not necessarily more generalizable than concrete ones. It is more fruitful, we suggest, to focus on *specific* dimensions of abstraction, and evaluate empirically how they affect the results researchers obtain. In the next section, we summarize the design of eight experiments we fielded – where we manipulate levels of situational hypotheticality, actor identity, and contextual detail – to determine if and how different forms of abstraction shape experimental results. Readers interested in

---

[8] This is true both for contextual treatment heterogeneity in which treatment effects vary with fea-tures of the situation not being modeled in the study (e.g., do the treatment effects in a relatively abstract scenario reflect the treatment effect for an "average" country?), and in respondent-level treatment heterogeneity, in which the treatment effects in the real world vary with characteristics of respondents that would not manifest themselves in a highly stylized scenario.

diving straight into our theoretical expectations and findings for each of these three dimensions can jump ahead to Sections 4, 5, and 6.

3 Methodological Overview

To provide guidance for experimentalists on how abstract their experiments *ought* to be as well as how scholars should balance the potential tradeoffs associated with differing levels of abstraction, we fielded a series of eight survey experiments, each designed to address the dimensions of abstraction described in the previous section. In this section, we discuss the design of each of these experiments, some of which build on prominent recent vignette survey experiments across a number of subfields of political science, and others of which are original experiments building off of prominent events in the news at the time the studies were fielded.

We begin by discussing the design of our five extension experiments, summarized in Table 3. These studies build off of Nicholson's (2012) study of elite cues in American immigration policy debates (hereafter referred to as the ELITE CUES experiment), Press, Sagan, and Valentino's (2013) test of the nuclear taboo in public opinion toward the use of force (the NUCLEAR WEAPONS experiment), Mutz and Kim's (2017) exploration of the role of in-group favoritism in trade preferences (the IN-GROUP FAVORITISM experiment) and two different versions of Tomz and Weeks' (2013) DEMOCRATIC PEACE experiment. Replicating and extending these studies, which hail from a range of subfields in political science, lets us ask how the conclusions the original articles drew would have differed had they employed different experimental design choices.

We then discuss the design of three original studies (summarized in Table 4), each of which borrows from highly salient real-world events to further explore the consequences of different types of situational hypotheticality in particular. Our VICE PRESIDENT experiment explores the dynamics of American public opinion about Joe Biden's selection of a vice-presidential candidate (fielded before the then-Democratic presidential candidate had chosen Kamala Harris as his running mate), with the central substantive treatment focused on the race of the vice-presidential nominee. Our PROTEST experiment explores how Americans think about domestic protests (fielded as Black Lives Matter protests swept across the United States in the aftermath of the murder of George Floyd) by manipulating whether the protestors were described as engaging in either peaceful demonstrations or "vandalism, looting and violent actions." Finally, our WORLD HEALTH ORGANIZATION experiment examines attitudes toward US involvement in the World Health Organization (WHO) (fielded as the Trump administration considered pulling out of the international organization in the midst of the global pandemic). In this last study, the central substantive treatment is whether or not the United States withdraws from or remains in the WHO.

We conclude the section by presenting the findings for the substantive treatments for each of these eight experiments. The purpose of this analysis is twofold. First, while our main interest in the Element is methodological rather than substantive (what are the consequences of different types of abstraction in survey experiments?), beginning the analysis by focusing on the substantive treatments makes the discussion more concrete in the sections that follow. That said, each of the sections that follow is designed to be self-contained, such that readers can also skip ahead to Sections 4–6 if they wish, which present our results for situational hypotheticality, actor identity, and contextual detail, respectively. Second, for the extension experiments, we show that when we subset our data to the levels of abstraction that resemble those selected in the original studies, we replicate the original findings. This increases our confidence in the analysis that follows in subsequent sections.

3.1 About the Studies

The eight experiments discussed were fielded in two sets of studies. The Nuclear Weapons and In-Group Favoritism experiments were fielded on a sample of $N=4,686$ respondents through Dynata in spring 2019. The Elite Cues experiment was fielded along with the three original studies – Protest, Vice-President and World Health Organization – on a sample of $N=4,070$ respondents through Lucid's "Theorem" respondent pool in spring 2020. The Democratic Peace study was fielded in both waves, with small differences described in Section 3.2.[9] The order of experiments within each set of studies was randomized to guard against potential order effects.

3.2 Replications and Extensions

As Table 3 shows, our replication-based studies were designed with four levels of treatments:

1. the substantive treatments from the replicated studies
2. contextual detail treatments varying the amount of context respondents were presented

---

[9] More details, including the survey instruments themselves, and sample demographics, are available in Appendix §1.

3. actor identity treatments varying the names of the actors respondents were presented

4. a situational hypotheticality treatment – describing experimental scenarios as either explicitly real, explicitly hypothetical, or not mentioning hypotheticality at all – assigned at the respondent level

An additional summary of the structure of our survey instrument is depicted in Appendix §1. The situational hypotheticality treatments were randomized at the respondent level rather than the study level, so if a respondent was assigned to the explicit hypothetical treatment, all of the vignettes they saw would be described similarly. In our IN-GROUP FAVORITISM AND NUCLEAR WEAPONS studies, respondents were assigned to one of two conditions describing a situation as either explicitly hypothetical ("a hypothetical situation…") or more ambiguously described as "a situation." Our first DEMOCRATIC PEACE study also utilized the same two hypotheticality treatments, while the second version, DEMOCRATIC PEACE II, and our ELITE CUES study added a condition in which the situation was explicitly described as "real." The details of the three individual studies are set out in this section, and depicted in Table 3.

Elite Cues Experiment: Manipulating Actor Identity

In our extension of Nicholson's (2012) study we focus on a common dilemma for experimental political scientists: whether to name specific actors – whether politicians, countries, or organizations – in a vignette or leave them unspecified, and if the actors are named, whether they should be highly recognizable, relatively low-salience, or made up from scratch. Nicholson (2012) uses immigration as a case for exploring how citizens' political attitudes are affected by endorsements from politicians from inside versus outside their own political party. His original study examined the effect of in/out party endorsements on public opinion in the context of a proposal to reform US immigration policy that centered on a "path to citizenship" and used high-salience real actors: Barack Obama or John McCain. In our replication, we updated the relevant salient cuegivers (Joe Biden or Donald Trump), while also adding additional actor identity treatments that vary whether the immigration reform endorsement is made by less salient partisan cuegivers (Senator Tom Carper of Delaware or Senator Mike Rounds of South Dakota), or by a fictional politician (Stephen Smith) whose partisanship we manipulate. Additionally, we update the substantive context of the experiment to focus on protection for "Dreamers" in the United States.

Our procedure for our ELITE CUES replication is detailed in Appendix §2.1. Like Nicholson, we present respondents with an experimental scenario in which

Table 3 Summary of treatments for extension studies

	Elite Cues: Nicholson 2012	In-Group Favoritism: Mutz and Kim 2017	Nuclear Weapons: Press, Sagan, and Valentino 2013	Democratic Peace: Tomz, and Weeks 2013
Treatments from original study	1. No Endorsement 2. In-Party Cue 3. Out-Party Cue	1. US gains 1,000 and other country gains 10 2. US gains 10 and other country gains 1,000 3. US gains 10 and other country loses 1,000	1. 45% Success for conventional attack 2. 90% Success for conventional attack	1. Democracy 2. Not a Democracy
Actor identity treatments	If assigned to cue: 1. Real + High Salience (Donald Trump/ Joe Biden) 2. Real + Low Salience (Mike Rounds/ Tom Carper) 3. Fictional (Stephen Smith/ Stephen Smith)	—	1. Unnamed (foreign country) 2. Made up (Malaguay) 3. Real (Syria) 4. Real (Bolivia)	1. Unnamed (foreign country) (*I* and *II*) 2. Made up (Malaguay) (*I* only) 3. Real (Iran) (*I* and *II*) 4. Real (Ecuador) (*I* only) 5. Real (Turkey) (*II* only)

Table 3 *(cont.)*

	Elite Cues: Nicholson 2012	In-Group Favoritism: Mutz and Kim 2017	Nuclear Weapons: Press, Sagan, and Valentino 2013	Democratic Peace: Tomz, and Weeks 2013
Contextual detail treatments	—	1. No Additional Context (original) 2. Filler Context 3. Charged Context	1. Extended Context (original) 2. Reduced context	—
Situational hypotheticality treatment	Situation described as: 1. A situation 2. Explicitly hypothetical 3. Real	Situation described as: 1. A situation 2. Explicitly hypothetical	Situation described as: 1. A situation 2. Explicitly hypothetical	Situation described as: 1. A situation (*I* and *II*) 2. Explicitly hypothetical (*I* and *II*) 3. Real (*II* only)
Fielded:	Lucid, 2020	Dynata, 2019	Dynata, 2019	*I*: Dynata, 2019 *II*: Lucid, 2020
Factorial design:	$(1 \times 3) + (2 \times 3 \times 3) = 21$	$3 \times 3 \times 2 = 18$	$2 \times 2 \times 4 \times 2 = 32$	*I*: $2 \times 4 \times 2 = 16$ *II*: $2 \times 3 \times 3 = 18$

information is presented about an immigration reform policy "in the news." The situation was described as simply a "a situation" (making no mention of hypotheticality), "a hypothetical situation" (an explicit invocation of hypotheticality), or referred to as "a real situation." Depending on which treatment arm they were assigned to, respondents also read that the proposal was backed by either Donald Trump, Joe Biden, Mike Rounds, Tom Carper, or Stephen Smith – or did not receive any additional information about endorsements. The actor identity treatments were designed to randomize the salience of the actors (whether low or high, for example comparing Mike Rounds and Tom Carper to Donald Trump and Joe Biden) and whether or not they were real or fictional (as in Stephen Smith). In each condition, respondents were told whether the endorser was a Republican or Democrat and for the fictional endorser the partisan affiliation was randomized. Respondents then answered our outcome measure – "What is your view of this immigration policy?" – coded such that higher values mean greater opposition toward the policy. Following the outcome measure, respondents completed a manipulation check (asking whether the policy was endorsed by a member of a given political party or not endorsed by anyone). The inclusion of this item enables us to determine in later sections how actor identities affect respondents' comprehension and recall of the substantive treatment.

In-Group Favoritism Experiment: Manipulating Contextual Detail

Mutz and Kim (2017) use a survey experiment to examine the impact of in-group favoritism on American attitudes toward international trade by randomizing the expected US gains and losses from a trade agreement in comparison to another country. Their study therefore asks to what extent support for trade is shaped by whether respondents believe their country is "winning" more in the agreement than their trading partner is.[10] In extending upon their basic framework, we focus on a common decision experimentalists grapple with when designing instruments: How much contextual detail should vignettes include? Should they be stripped-down, bare-bones vignettes that highlight salient factors, or context-rich stories that in their level of detail more closely resemble the volume of information we might encounter in our daily lives? We do so by randomly assigning respondents to either the original short vignette (about 55 words, depending on the substantive treatment condition), or a more lengthy vignette (about 240 words) which provides further detail on the experimental scenario. Consistent with Bansak and colleagues (2021), we provide two types

---

[10] See also Brutger and Rathbun (2021).

of additional context. The first is "filler" context, peripheral information that increases the volume of text respondents are presented with, but is not expected to interact with the treatment. The second is "charged" context that similarly increases the length of the stimulus, but which is more relevant to the treatment. In so doing, we test how additional information that is either likely or unlikely to interact with the study's main treatment moderates the original findings.

In particular, when implementing our study, we consider how providing respondents with increased context moderates the main identified treatment effect. Thus we manipulate the context in the experimental vignette to include either: (1) no additional context, (2) filler context, which is *unlikely* to interact with treatment, or (3) charged context, which is *likely* to interact with treatment. Apart from our contextual detail treatment, we follow a simplified version of the procedure implemented in Mutz and Kim (2017). The main treatment from the original study is a description of the effects of a trade policy, which is described as either:

1. For each 1,000 people in the United States who gain a job and can now provide for their family, 10 people in a country that we trade with will gain new jobs and now be able to provide for their family.
2. For each 10 people in the United States who gain a job and can now provide for their family, 1,000 people in a country that we trade with will gain new jobs and now be able to provide for their family.
3. For each 10 people in the United States who gain a job and can now provide for their family, 1,000 people in a country that we trade with will lose their jobs and will no longer be able to provide for their family.

The vignette itself is introduced briefly and randomized between a version that is either explicitly hypothetical or ambiguously described as "a situation." The outcome measure for this study is support for the trade policy described ("Would you be likely to support this trade policy or oppose this trade policy?," followed by questions gauging whether respondents are strongly or somewhat opposed/supportive of the policy). In the analysis that follows, we combine the latter two conditions to form a pooled control, such that the substantive treatment effect can be interpreted as the effect of the US experiencing large relative gains from trade.

A detailed description of our replication protocol for our IN-GROUP FAVORITISM study is provided in Appendix §2.2. In a similar fashion to our ELITE CUES study, we include a manipulation check, which lets us test whether increased contextual detail affects respondents' comprehension of experimental scenarios and treatments.

Democratic Peace Experiment: Manipulating Situational Hypotheticality and Actor Identity

In our DEMOCRATIC PEACE experiment, we replicate Tomz and Weeks' (2013) influential study investigating the effects of knowing a target country is a democracy on respondents' willingness to support the use of force against it.[11] The original study measured the extent to which US and UK respondents' preferences for military strikes were affected by the regime type of a country that was described as developing nuclear weapons. We fielded two different extensions of this study, DEMOCRATIC PEACE I in 2019, and DEMOCRATIC PEACE II in 2020.

The original study used a factorial experiment, but for the sake of simplicity in our extensions, we manipulated only the main democracy treatment, holding other treatment arms (e.g., alliance status and levels of trade) constant. The democracy treatment described the country developing nuclear weapons as being "a democracy and showing every sign that it will remain a democracy" or "not a democracy and showing no sign of becoming a democracy."

Our contribution in this extension is to add several additional features, allowing us to examine actor identity (as in our ELITE CUES study) and situational hypotheticality. In DEMOCRATIC PEACE I, the survey vignette was introduced as either *explicitly* hypothetical ("We are now going to describe to you a hypothetical situation") or left ambiguous ("We are now going to describe to you a situation"). In DEMOCRATIC PEACE II, we included both hypotheticality treatments and added an explicitly "real" treatment, telling respondents: "We are now going to describe to you a real situation the United States is facing."

For our actor identity treatments, we consider the empirical consequences of a range of different choices that researchers can make relating to country names. These include:

1. leaving the country name unnamed ("a country")
2. utilizing a fictitious or made up country name ("Malaguay")
3. utilizing a real country that is schema consistent and treatment inconsistent (Iran)
4. utilizing a real country that is schema consistent and treatment consistent (Turkey)
5. utilizing a real country that is schema inconsistent (Ecuador)

---

[11] For other experimental studies of the democratic peace, see Mintz and Geva (1993); Johns and Davies (2012).

In Section 5, we discuss what we mean by schema and treatment consistency in greater detail: schema consistency refers to the extent to which the actor selected (and held constant across treatment arms) is consistent with other theoretically-relevant features of the scenario, and treatment consistency refers to the degree of compatibility between the actor selected and the levels of the treatments being manipulated. Section 5 also presents the results of a pretest we conducted to determine which countries fall into which category. The outcome measure for this study was "Would you favor or oppose using the US military to attack *the country's / Malaguay's / Iran's / Turkey's / Ecuador's* nuclear development sites?" Response options ranged from 1 (oppose strongly) to 5 (favor strongly). Respondents also received a manipulation check, asking them to think back to the scenario described earlier and indicate whether the country with which the United States was engaging was a democracy or not.

Nuclear Weapons Experiment: Manipulating Both Contextual Detail and Actor Identity

In our NUCLEAR WEAPONS study, we replicate Press, Sagan, and Valentino's (2013) experiment on "atomic aversion." Their study probes the existence of a taboo against nuclear weapons use (e.g., Tannenwald, 1999) in the mass public, by presenting respondents with a scenario where the United States is considering either a conventional weapons attack or a nuclear attack, manipulating the relative efficacy of nuclear weapons, and testing how it affects the rate at which respondents choose the nuclear attack. The original study presented respondents with a lengthy vignette describing a report from the Joint Chiefs to the President characterizing conventional weapons as either being *equally effective* as nuclear weapons in their likelihood of destroying a potential target, or half as likely to be effective as a nuclear attack would be.[12] Following presenting respondents with the scenario, we administer our outcome measure of interest: "If you had to choose between one of the two US military options described in the article, would you prefer the nuclear strike or the conventional strike?," with an ordinal scale in which higher values indicate stronger support for the nuclear option.

In our extension, we examine the joint effects of contextual detail, situational hypotheticality, and actor identity, adding three additional treatment arms to the original study. More specifically, we manipulate the vignette's context to either

---

[12] The original study includes three treatment conditions where conventional attacks have a 90, 70, or 45 percent success probability in relation to nuclear attacks which are held constant at 90 percent probability of success. The original study also randomizes whether the scenario is described as prospective or retrospective. For the sake of simplicity we only consider the 90 and 45 percent success probability conditions, and we described scenarios as prospective.

include: (1) elaborate context (replicating the context presented in the original study, which presented respondents with a lengthy news article of about 520 words, depending on the substantive treatment) or (2) reduced context - cutting the vignette in half, to about 250 words. We also randomize the name of the country presented in the scenario:

1. A real country, schema consistent and treatment consistent (Syria, which was also used in the original study)
2. An unnamed country ("a foreign country")
3. A fictitious country name ("Malaguay")
4. A real and schema-inconsistent and treatment-consistent country (Bolivia)

In Section 5, we further elaborate on schema and treatment consistency, and present the results of a pretest used to determine which country names were manipulated here.

Finally, in our extension we also randomize explicit hypotheticality, presenting respondents with a version of the scenario that is either left ambiguous or explicitly hypothetical. As detailed in Appendix §2.3, apart from our two additional treatment arms and the simplification of original treatments, we follow a similar procedure to Press, Sagan, and Valentino. Respondents were also presented with a factual manipulation check gauging the extent to which they recalled the substantive treatment.

3.3 Original Studies

Our original studies – VICE-PRESIDENT, PROTEST, and WORLD HEALTH ORGANIZATION – largely focused on the dimension of situational hypotheticality. All three issues – US involvement in the World Health Organization during the COVID-19 pandemic, protests regarding racial justice, and the selection of a female vice-presidential candidate – were highly salient issues during the time the studies were fielded (June 2020). Since all three experiments focus on real-world events that were relatively salient at the time of the studies' fielding, we manipulated situational hypotheticality in different ways across the studies: explicitly calling the scenario hypothetical, making it more abstract by setting it in the future, and an additional treatment where we attempt to make the future scenario seem less hypothetical by emphasizing that experts indicate this type of scenario is likely to occur in the future. In the PROTEST study, we also included a condition in which no mention of hypotheticality or the future is present. Treatments for our original studies are summarized in Table 4. After the main outcome measure for each study, we presented respondents with a thought listing exercise and factual questions relating to the substantive treatment.

Table 4 Summary of original studies

	Protest	Vice-president	World Health Organization
Substantive treatment	Protest type: violent/peaceful demonstrations	Candidate race: White/African American	US behavior: United States withdraws from/remains in WHO
DV	Support for protests	Likelihood of voting for candidate	1. trust in WHO 2. WHO good or bad for the United States.
Situational hypotheticality treatment	Situation described as: 1. hypothetical 2. future 3. expert prediction 4. a situation	Situation described as: 1. hypothetical 2. future 3. expert prediction	Situation described as: 1. hypothetical 2. future 3. expert prediction
Factorial Design	$2 \times 3 = 6$	$2 \times 4 = 8$	$2 \times 3 = 6$

Protest Experiment

Our PROTEST study was designed around real-world events in the United States during the time of fielding, eliciting respondent attitudes on a subject that respondents would likely have heard or thought about in their daily lives. Respondents read that "thousands of people across the United States have participated in protests, demanding racial justice and condemning police brutality." The protestors were then described engaging in either "vandalism, looting, and violent action" or "peaceful demonstrations which avoid vandalism and looting." Our dependent variable in this study was agreement with the statement "I support the cause of the protests which are demanding racial justice and an end to police brutality." In this sense, this experiment is consistent with other recent work exploring the effect of protesters' tactics on the public's evaluations of protesters and their cause (e.g., Huff and Kruszewska, 2016; Hsiao and Radnitz, 2021; Edwards and Arnon, 2021; Green-Riley, Kruszewska-Eduardo, and Fu, 2021).

Situational hypotheticality was manipulated in our preamble to the vignette. In some cases, mimicking a common method in political science, the scenario was introduced as a "hypothetical scenario." In another treatment arm, the vignette was described as a "scenario that may happen in the future" and began "It is the year 2030…" In our third treatment arm, any mention of the future or "hypotheticality" was eliminated and subjects were simply asked to consider the scenario, with an addendum that "political experts and commentators expect that protests will engage in…" either violent or peaceful demonstrations. Our last treatment arm simply asked respondents to "consider the following scenario…" and described actions that protests were taking as ones that "protesters are engaging in."

Vice President Experiment

In the VICE-PRESIDENT study, we describe a scenario surrounding an election and focused on the selection of a female vice-presidential running mate by a Democratic candidate for US president. The substantive treatment for the study was whether the female nominee for vice president was described as white or African-American – building on a longer tradition of experiments in American politics interested in testing the effects of race on candidate evaluation (e.g., Mendelberg, 2001; Wamble, 2020). Situational hypotheticality – treated at the respondent level – was experimentally manipulated so that the election (and the selection of the candidate) was described as either:

1. hypothetical: a "hypothetical presidential race,"
2. expert: "As part of the upcoming 2020 presidential race, leading political experts expect…"
3. future: "in the 2028 presidential race."

Like the PROTEST experiment, then, the VICE-PRESIDENT experiment lets us turn the question of situational hypotheticality on its head, not investigating whether invoking hypotheticality causes respondents to tune out or not take the study seriously, but rather, whether taking events ripped from the headlines and cloaking them under the guise of hypotheticality actually causes respondents to give different answers than they would when the scenario is explicitly about these current events.

Our outcome measure for this study was respondents' stated likelihood of voting for the candidate ("How likely are you to vote for this candidate?," scaled from 1-5). Following the outcome measure, subjects completed a thought-listing task ("When you think about the scenario you just read, what features or details of the scenario come to mind?"), a manipulation check asking about the identity of the vice-presidential candidate, and a question asking if any particular real-world politician came to mind when reading the experimental vignette.

World Health Organization Experiment

Our third original study focused on US involvement in the WHO. It began by noting that "There has been much discussion about levels of United States' support for the World Health Organization (WHO) and the United States' continued role in the organization." The substantive treatment varies whether the United States has decided to either leave or remain in the WHO. In this sense, the study is similar to other recent work that explores public opinion about exit from international organizations (e.g., von Borzyskowski and Vabulas, 2021). Our outcome measure for this study captures respondents' degree of support for or confidence in the WHO, asking respondents the extent to which they agree with the statement "I trust the World Health Organization to do what is right." As in the VICE-PRESIDENT study, situational hypotheticality was manipulated in three ways: a version of the vignette described as hypothetical, a version set in the future, and a version set in the present time in which it was noted that "political experts expected" the decision to stay in or leave the WHO to occur in a few days.

3.4 Effects of Substantive Treatments

While Sections 4–6 present the results of our abstraction manipulations in detail, here we briefly discuss the effects of the substantive treatments in each study. In Figure 1 we present the results for the substantive treatments in the five extension experiments – subsetting the data to the treatment combinations that most closely resembled the type of abstraction used in the original experiments – as well as our original studies.[13] In the lower portion of the figure, we plot the substantive treatment effect in our IN-GROUP FAVORITISM study of trade and in-group preferences.

As shown in Figure 1, respondents in the treatment condition are much more likely to support trade deals when the United States is expected to gain more ($p<0.01$).[14]

In the middle region of Figure 1, we present our ELITE CUES replication focused on immigration-policy endorsements. Specifically, we consider how exposing partisans to out-party cues supporting a given immigration reform affects opposition for the named reform. As evident from the study's original data (depicted with circles), as well as our replication (depicted using triangles), out-party endorsement cues have a positive effect on opposition to the immigration policy.[15] Notably effect sizes are comparable in the original study and our replication.

The third set of estimates come from our NUCLEAR WEAPONS replication. Here, we test whether exposing respondents to a vignette in which a nuclear attack is more effective than a conventional attack alters support rates for nuclear attacks. As evident, we replicate Press, Sagan, and Valentino's initial results, demonstrating that respondents are more likely to support a nuclear attack when it is described as more effective than a conventional attack.[16]

Our set of results at the top of the plot depict estimates from our two DEMOCRATIC PEACE studies, as well as the original study results (depicted using a circle), showing that, in both cases, opposition to the use of force increases when the target is a democracy.[17] Taken together, the results in Figure 1

---

[13] In the ELITE CUES experiment, we restrict the analysis to high-salience actors; in the IN-GROUP FAVORITISM experiment we restrict the analysis to no additional context; in the DEMOCRATIC PEACE experiments, we restrict the analysis to the unnamed country condition; in the NUCLEAR WEAPONS experiment, we restrict the analysis to the extended context and Syria conditions. For the original studies, we display the average treatment effect averaging over the other treatment dimensions. In Appendix §8 we examine potential interactions of treatments and the cumulative effect of multiple forms of abstraction.

[14] We do not include the original data estimate for the IN-GROUP FAVORITISM experiment because the original study included a more elaborate design; we also utilize a slightly different estimation strategy as in the original ELITE CUES experiment. Importantly, however, our results remain the same.

[15] $p<0.1$ for the original study and $p<0.01$ for our replication. For ease of interpretation, in these analyses we compare respondents receiving in-party cues with respondents receiving out-party cues, omitting all respondents in the no-cue condition.

[16] $p<0.01$ in the original study and $p<0.01$ in our replication.

[17] $p<0.01$ for DEMOCRATIC PEACE I, $p<0.01$ for II, and $p<0.01$ for the original.

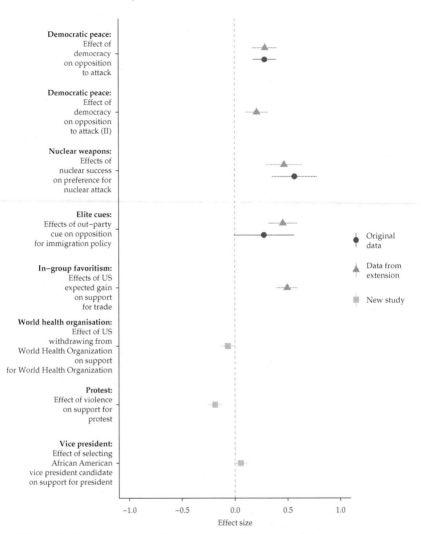

Figure 1 Treatment effects from the extensions and original experiments

Figure 1 shows we successfully identify the average treatment effects of all studies under investigation. Point estimates and corresponding 95 percent confidence intervals are extracted from separate OLS models where original outcomes are predicted by treatments. When possible we benchmark our replication (triangles) to original studies (circles). In doing so, we consider respondents exposed to the original format of the experiment, omitting respondents exposed to new variants of the experiment where we introduce diverging elements of abstraction or detail. All outcomes are standardized.

demonstrate our broad success in replicating our studies of interest, increasing the credibility of the extensions we present in the subsequent sections.

The bottom portion of Figure 1 presents the substantive treatment effects for our original studies. The bottom row presents the results from our

VICE-PRESIDENT experiment, showing that respondents become more support-ive ($p<0.1$) of the presidential nominee when the nominee selects a Black candidate to serve as their running-mate. The middle row presents the results from our PROTEST experiment, showing that support for the protesters' cause drops ($p<0.01$) when the protesters are described as using violent tactics. The top row presents the results from our WORLD HEALTH ORGANIZATION experi-ment, showing that respondents become less supportive of the WHO ($p<0.05$) when the United States withdraws.

3.5 Conclusion

This section presented a big-picture overview of the designs of the eight sur-vey experiments we fielded to investigate abstraction in experimental design. Some of these studies replicate and extend prominent recent survey experi-ments from a range of subfields of political science, while others are original designs studying political dynamics in the news at the time the studies were fielded. The section also briefly presented the results of the substantive treat-ments in each of these studies, showing that we are able to replicate the findings of the original experiments the extensions are based on, thereby increasing our confidence in the results. In the next three sections we turn to our central quan-tities of interest: to what extent does varying situational hypotheticality, actor identity, and contextual detail change the results that experimenters obtain?

4 Situational Hypotheticality

Experimentalists often wrestle with a challenge: we turn to experiments to identify causal effects, and causation often requires manipulation (Holland, 1986), but there are limits to what experimentalists can credibly manipulate. Some experiments intervene by treating respondents with information about the world that they might not otherwise have (e.g., Butler, Nickerson et al., 2011; Raffler, 2019), but especially in survey experiments, experimentalists often manipulate features of the world itself, presenting respondents with alter-nate realities: where politicians say and do things they might not have yet said or done (e.g., Tomz, 2007), or events take place that have not yet transpired (e.g., Lyall, Blair, and Imai, 2013).

Experimenters seeking to manipulate reality in this way typically have a number of different options, which we can array on a rough continuum of hypo-theticality. At one end of the continuum, one way researchers can justify why the scenario being described to respondents deviates from the reality respon-dents face is to explicitly describe a scenario as being hypothetical, although sometimes scholars express concern that respondents do not take hypothetical questions seriously (e.g., Mutz, 2011, 59). At the other end of the continuum, experiments can attempt to eschew hypotheticality by using deception, telling respondents that a (fictional) scenario is real. Finally, in the middle of the continuum are a number of other options experimenters often take if they don't want to use deception, but are worried that explicit invocations of hypotheticality might cause respondents to disengage from the scenario. In these cases, experimenters leave the scenario's hypotheticality ambiguous by merely referring to a "situation" – not explicitly telling respondents that a scenario is real, but not calling it hypothetical either (e.g., Chapman and Chaudoin, 2020). Another similar strategy is to set the scenario in the future – not saying the scenario has happened, but rather, merely that it could happen (e.g., Mattes and Weeks, 2019). Researchers can also lend further credibility to these prospective scenarios by invoking experts who indicate that the scenario described by the experimenter is likely to occur (e.g., Bassan-Nygate and Weiss, 2022; Tankard and Paluck, 2017). To what extent do these different experimental design choices affect the results that researchers obtain?

There are a number of reasons why we might expect these design choices to be consequential, two of which are flagged by Mutz (2021). The first is in terms of motivation: if respondents find hypothetical choices less engaging, they are less likely to take the study seriously. The second is in terms of information processing: psychological frameworks like construal level theory, for example, argue that individuals reason more abstractly about hypothetical decisions. We have stronger reactions to real events than hypothetical ones, and when we consider hypothetical questions, we are more likely to focus on higher-level dimensions rather than specific details, privileging the desirability of an outcome rather than its feasibility (Trope and Liberman, 2010). Huddleston (2019) applies this framework to foreign policy public opinion experiments in political science, arguing that the hypothetical nature of many foreign policy experiments causes respondents to discount costs. For these reasons, Mutz (2021, 232) expresses concern about the frequency of hypothetical scenarios in political science experiments, noting that "to the extent that we want people to process experimental stimuli as if they were real, this is obviously problematic."

In this section, we present evidence from eight experiments (ELITE CUES, IN-GROUP FAVORITISM, NUCLEAR WEAPONS, the WORLD HEALTH ORGANIZATION, PROTEST, VICE PRESIDENT, and two different iterations of DEMOCRATIC PEACE, all of which are described in detail in Section 3), which test the moderating effect of situational hypotheticality on the experiments' substantive treatment effects. Although experimentalists in political science often go to great lengths to avoid using the word "hypothetical," we find little evidence that explicit hypotheticality moderates the results in the studies shown here. This matters in as much as sometimes researchers feel like they need to deceive respondents in order to ensure they take the study seriously. Our results suggest that this deception may not be necessary.

It is worth clarifying what we do not do. In particular, the studies do not compare survey experiment results with behavioral benchmarks in field experiment contexts (e.g., Findley, Nielson, and Sharman, 2013), or test whether the attitudes expressed in these experimental contexts manifest themselves similarly in real-world choices (e.g., Hainmueller, Hangartner, and Yamamoto, 2015). What they do suggest is that when researchers field survey experiments, the degree of situational hypotheticality featured in the experimental vignette does not significantly affect the results that experimenters obtain.

4.1 Using Deception

We begin with the starkest modeling choice, comparing the options at the two poles of the hypotheticality continuum: explicitly calling the experimental scenario hypothetical (as in Boettcher 2004, 344, for example, who asks respondents to "envision a hypothetical presidency apart from the current administration"), versus explicitly calling a scenario real. The use of deception in experiments can be controversial, depending on the field of research and the type of deception being employed (Hertwig and Ortmann, 2008). In psychology deception is widely used in experimental designs, whereas in economics it is forbidden by some of the top journals (Rousu et al., 2015). In political science, deception is formally allowed by almost all journals and IRBs (Yanow and Schwartz-Shea, 2016), though in our experiences we have found that some reviewers have an instinctive aversion to studies that employ deception. Given the debates around deception, many scholars prefer to avoid using deception in their designs, but also worry about reducing their experimental control or generalizability if they present a hypothetical scenario (Mutz, 2011, 59).

Researchers who are concerned about the potential risks of using hypothetical scenarios sometimes choose to present their experiments as real, even if that means using deception. This has often been justified by arguing that certain situations do not occur readily in the real world and thus experiments must deceive the respondent to evaluate the effects of variables that may not readily occur in natural settings (Hertwig and Ortmann, 2008). This is also an empirical question, however, which we evaluate using the ELITE CUES and second DEMOCRATIC PEACE experiment. In these studies, before presenting respondents with details of the scenario, a random subset of respondents were told they were being given a "hypothetical scenario," while another random subset were told the scenario they were being presented with was real.

In Figure 2 (as in all the figures that follow), we present the results of the original treatment from a given study at different levels of hypotheticality, as well as presenting the results from an OLS model where we interact this study-level treatment with our hypotheticality treatment.[18] Thus, for the ELITE CUES experiment, for example, Figure 2 shows the effects of an out-party politician being the endorser of the immigration reform policy if the scenario is described as real, versus as explicitly hypothetical. In both experiments, our analysis suggests that invoking explicit hypotheticality generates substantively similar results as when scenarios are described as real.[19] This suggests that concerns about presenting scenarios as hypothetical (rather than real) are likely overblown. Furthermore, in many cases using deception may not be necessary.

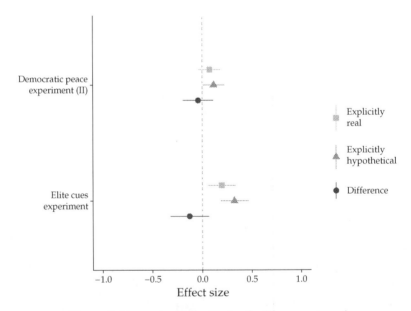

Figure 2 No moderating effects of calling events real

Figure 2 finds that describing an experiment as real rather than explicitly hypothetical does not moderate average treatment effects.

---

[18] In all the figures in this section, point estimates are shown with 95 percent confidence intervals, and all outcomes are standardized for ease of comparability.

[19] p value for interaction in DEMOCRATIC PEACE II=.534, and for interaction in ELITE CUES=.195)

4.2 Explicit versus Ambiguous Hypotheticality

Another modeling choice concerns whether to leave the hypotheticality ambiguous, presenting respondents with a situation without indicating its veracity. This modeling choice is used frequently in the experimental literature. Kriner and Shen (2014) do not use the word "hypothetical," but tell respondents to "Imagine for a moment that a future President has decided to ..." carry out a series of actions, clearly implicating hypotheticality. Tomz and Weeks (2013), Bell and Quek (2018), Yarhi-Milo, Kertzer, and Renshon (2018), and Bush and Zetterberg (2021) all describe "a situation" that respondents' countries have faced in the past, and could face again in the future. To what extent do these modeling choices affect the results experimentalists obtain?

To assess the impact of these choices, we present results from the two DEMOCRATIC PEACE experiments, the IN-GROUP FAVORITISM experiment, the NUCLEAR WEAPONS experiment, and the ELITE CUES experiment. In these studies, a random subset of respondents were told they were being given a "hypothetical scenario," while another random subset were simply given a "scenario," whose hypotheticality was left ambiguous. Figure 3 compares the explicit hypotheticality versus ambiguous hypotheticality results, showing that across all five of these experiments, there is little evidence that respondents are allergic to the word hypothetical: respondents do not respond to the study-level treatments significantly differently when told that the scenario is explicitly hypothetical versus left ambiguous.[20]

4.3 Moving Current Events into the Future and Invoking Experts

One possibility, however, might be that the effects of explicit hypotheticality might be more pronounced in experiments that relate to current events. This concern is manifested in the proliferation of vignettes in survey experiments in political science that make clear that "the scenario" that respondents are being presented with "is not about a specific event in the news today" (e.g., Tomz and Weeks, 2013; Mattes and Weeks, 2019; Bush and Zetterberg, 2021), a deliberate effort to prevent respondents from anchoring their answers too heavily on current events.

To explore the consequences of these approaches, we present results from the VICE PRESIDENT, PROTEST, and WORLD HEALTH ORGANIZATION experiments. As Section 3 notes, all three of these experiments pertained to events in the news at the time the studies were fielded: President Biden's deliberations about

---

[20] *p* value for interactions: DEMOCRATIC PEACE I=.590, DEMOCRATIC PEACE II=.890, NUCLEAR WEAPONS=.600, IN-GROUP FAVORITISM=.134, ELITE CUES=.958.

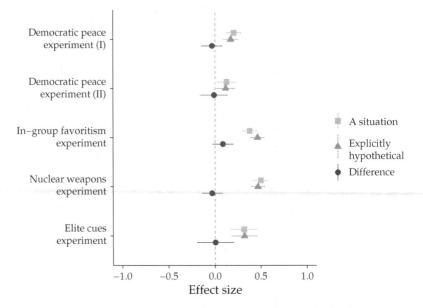

Figure 3 No moderating effects of explicit hypotheticality

Figure 3 finds no evidence that explicitly invoking situational hypotheticality (rather than simply describing a "situation") significantly moderates our treatment effects in any of the five experiments.

selecting a vice-presidential nominee, Black Lives Matter protests that had gar-nered major media attention, both in the United States and around the world, and the Trump administration withdrawing from the World Health Organiza-tion. In these studies, a random subset of respondents were told they were being given a hypothetical scenario, while another random subset were given a sce-nario taking place in the future, therefore signaling to respondents that they weren't simply being asked about current events.

Figure 4 presents results from these studies, showing that in two of the three experiments (the VICE PRESIDENT experiment, and the WORLD HEALTH ORGANIZATION experiment), relocating events in the future does not signifi-cantly change the treatment effects experimenters recover. For the PROTEST experiment, there is evidence that the effect of violent (compared to nonvio-lent) tactics on support is weaker in the future scenario than the hypothetical scenario ($p<0.05$). We unpack the PROTEST result by walking through what the substantive effect means. The significant difference demonstrates that respon-dents were significantly less supportive of "demanding racial justice and an end to police brutality," in the violent protest treatment condition when the vignette was set in the year 2030, but the violent protest treatment did not sig-nificantly lower support in the other conditions. This suggests that respondents were more willing to embrace the cause of racial justice – even in the face

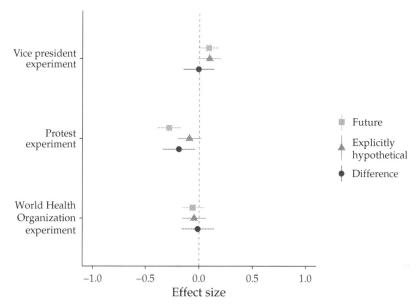

Figure 4 Limited moderating effects of locating events in the future

Figure 4 finds limited evidence that describing a situation as a future event (rather than an explicitly hypothetical event) can moderate average treatment effects.

of violent protests – when it was *not* temporally distant. Given that the Black Lives Matter movement was exceptionally salient at the time of the survey, our results are consistent with respondents supporting the cause of racial justice *now*, regardless of protest strategies, even if they were less likely to do so in a future hypothetical scenario, which may have seemed less urgent to respondents. However, since the effect of framing an experimental vignette in the future was not consistent across studies, we note that the signifiant difference for the PROTEST experiment result should be interpreted with caution.

We next examine how using expert projections as a means to make a situation more realistic affects experimental results. Scholars sometimes use this approach because it allows them to take current events and credibly manipulate their features. For example, some experts may predict that future protests will be largely peaceful, while others may predict that protests will be violent. Using expert projections may allow researchers to avoid using deception, while also providing a heightened sense of realism to the experiment. However, using expert projections not only places part of the scenario in the future, but also makes respondents think about experts' opinions, which may generate unintended reactions that are orthogonal to the treatment of interest.

In Figure 5 we assess the effect of using expert projections across the same three studies analyzed in Figure 4: the VICE PRESIDENT experiment, PROTEST

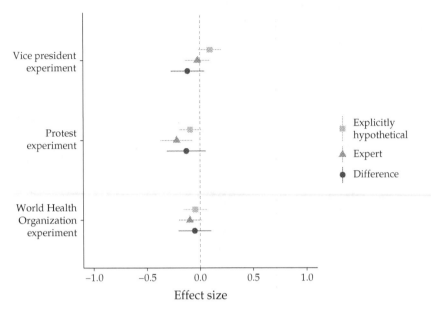

Figure 5 No moderating effects of invoking experts

Figure 5 finds that describing an experiment as a future event that experts foresee (rather than a hypothetical scenario), does not moderate average treatment effects.

experiment, and WORLD HEALTH ORGANIZATION experiment. As shown in the difference estimates, expert projections do not significantly moderate the substantive treatment effects in the experiments: we do not find any evidence that there are substantively different results when using an explicitly hypothetical scenario, versus a real scenario that uses expert projections to present the treatment.[21] Notably, in the PROTEST experiment, using expert projections did *not* moderate the treatment effect, unlike the results from Figure 4.

4.4 Conclusion

The accumulation of evidence from this section suggests that researchers have significant freedom to design their experiments as ambiguously or explicitly hypothetical, without jeopardizing the core results of their study. This means that, in many situations, researchers may be able to avoid using deception by explicitly telling respondents they are engaging with a hypothetical scenario, or the researcher may employ one of the various forms of hypotheticality we test here. Whether using real versus hypothetical scenarios, or turning to ambiguous versus explicit forms of hypotheticality, the substantive treatments

---

[21] *p* values for difference estimates: WORLD HEALTH ORGANIZATION =.520, VICE-PRESIDENT=. 150, PROTEST=.172.

experimenters obtain do not appear to significantly differ. It thus appears that the perceived benefits of using deception in order to present a scenario as real are far less than many have assumed.

Crucially, these experiments do not compare how respondents' behavior differs between hypothetical scenarios and real behavior. Each of the studies analyzed here focuses exclusively on attitudes toward politicians, political events, and policies, as opposed to behavioral outcomes such as voting, donations, or political engagement. Given that we know from existing research that stated and revealed preferences may diverge (Haas and Morton, 2018), and that people sometimes respond differently to hypothetical sums of money versus real amounts in decision games (e.g., Irwin, McClelland, and Schulze, 1992; Xu et al., 2018), we recognize the value of extending this research agenda to further explore how situational hypotheticality affects stated and revealed preferences, and whether the two interact in meaningful ways.

5 Actor Identities

When researchers design experimental scenarios, they often confront the question of what type of actors should populate their experiments. Sometimes experimenters select highly salient actors from the real world – politicians like Donald Trump or Joe Biden, or countries like China and India – who respondents are likely familiar with. Doing so may allow the the researcher to ground the experiment in attitudes toward specific real-world actors, which can provide studies with enhanced realism, but also raise concerns about generalizability, since the results obtained might be limited to the actors selected. Other times, experimenters include unnamed actors in experimental vignettes in order to enhance generalizability. At least implicitly, the selection of an unnamed actor is motivated by the assumption that a researcher's quantity of interest is a main, rather than a conditional, effect: the notion that researchers are interested in studying the effect of partisan cues on immigration attitudes more generally, rather than the effects of a message from Donald Trump on support for immigration from Afghanistan in particular, for example. This section seeks to shed new light on the questions of which actors to select for experiments and how we should think about the consequences of selecting certain types of actors for experimental designs.

We explore questions of actor identity in three types of experiments in particular. The first are survey experiments where the actor identity in question is fixed, and thus constitutes the setting or context in which a scenario is taking place. This is particularly common in survey experiments in international relations regarding support for the use of force, for example, in which experimenters indicate who the target of a military intervention or identity of a trading partner might be (e.g., Herrmann, Tetlock, and Visser, 1999; Guisinger, 2017; Mattes and Weeks, 2019), but the characteristics or identity of the actor is held constant and is not the central quantity of interest in the experiment itself. The second are survey experiments where the treatment manipulates *properties* of the actor, such as experiments in American or comparative politics manipulating the gender of political candidates (e.g., Huddy and Terkildsen, 1993; Matland and Tezcür, 2011; Schneider, 2014; Klar, 2018), or experiments in international relations manipulating characteristics of a country, such as its regime type or relative capabilities (e.g., Mintz and Geva, 1993; Rousseau and Garcia-Retamero, 2007; Tomz and Weeks, 2013). The third are endorsement or cue-giving experiments, which manipulate the *identity* of actors supporting or opposing a given policy and then measure public support for the policy in question (e.g., Druckman, Peterson, and Slothuus, 2013; Kertzer and Zeitzoff, 2017; Matanock and Garbiras-Díaz, 2018; Gadarian, Goodman, and Pepinsky, 2021). As we discuss in this section, we suggest that questions of actor identity can be particularly consequential for the latter two types of experiments, but are less so for experiments where the actor identity is orthogonal to the treatments themselves.

We argue that there are three factors in particular that experimenters should consider when choosing real-world actors. The first is *schema consistency* (Hashtroudi et al., 1984): In studies where the actor is fixed across treatment arms, is the choice of actor reasonable given the scenario in which the actor is embedded? If a schema-inconsistent actor is chosen, the respondent may be less likely to believe the scenario or accept the treatment, thus weakening the treatment effect. The second is *treatment consistency*: If the treatment manipulates an attribute of an actor, are all of the levels of the attribute being manipulated seen as plausible by respondents? If respondents do not perceive the treatment as consistent with the identity of the actor, then the experimenter is likely to lose control since the respondent may not comply with the treatment, attenuating the treatment effect. The third is the *salience* of the actor: when experimenters incorporate more prominent or well-known actors in their experiments, respondents are likely to have stronger prior attitudes or knowledge about the actor than when experimental scenarios feature actors about which respondents are unaware. Incorporating salient actors has important consequences for the magnitude of the treatment effects recovered, with the potential to increase the size of the treatment effects when the actor is embedded in the treatment (as in endorsement experiments), and the potential to decrease the size of the treatment effects when the actor is the object being evaluated (as in candidate evaluation experiments).

Drawing on five experiments, our findings suggest that concerns about schema consistency are perhaps overblown, but that treatment inconsistency can substantially weaken the treatment effects recovered. Experimenters designing studies where the attributes of actors are being manipulated may therefore wish to either generate artificial actors for the purpose of the experiment, or choose real-world actors where all levels of the treatment can be plausibly manipulated. Finally, in experiments about political candidates, we suggest that the use of salient actors can either strengthen or weaken treatment effects, depending on the design and quantity of interest of the study.

5.1 Schema versus Treatment Inconsistency

When experimenters choose real-world actors for their experiments, they are often choosing actors that respondents will have prior familiarity with. There are some contexts where experimenters deliberately place real-world actors in scenarios that are inconsistent with respondents' existing mental models, as in studies of whether political leaders can send more credible signals about the qualities of a policy by going against their "type" or brand (e.g., Trager and Vavreck, 2011; Saunders, 2018; Mattes and Weeks, 2019; Kertzer, Brooks, and Brooks, 2021): if respondents know that Fox News tends to be critical of Democratic political figures, and are presented with a story where commentators on Fox praise a policy decision carried out by Joe Biden, respondents may be more supportive of the policy decision in question, since out-party praise is more unexpected and thus more informative than out-party criticism or in-party praise (Baum and Groeling, 2009). If, however, there is incongruity between what respondents know about an actor and what they are being told in the experimental context, there is a risk respondents may not take the study seriously or believe the information presented. This incongruity can take two forms: one is schema inconsistency, where the choice of actor or setting of the experiment is inconsistent with other theoretically relevant features of the scenario in which respondents are presented (for example, a study about attitudes toward the use of force to halt a nuclear weapons program, which the experimenter is situating in Ecuador, a country not typically associated with nuclear proliferation).

The other type of incongruity is treatment inconsistency, where the experiment is actively manipulating features of the real-world actor, but not all levels of the treatment being assigned are seen as equally plausible by respondents (for example, a study manipulating Hilary Clinton's gender, or Barack Obama's race). It is because of a desire to avoid treatment inconsistency that studies of the effect of candidate race on candidate evaluation, for example, typically use hypothetical or fake political candidates (e.g., Wamble, 2020).

In this sense, both schema inconsistency and treatment inconsistency involve incongruities between features of the experiment and respondents' prior beliefs. However, since the incongruity in schema inconsistency is rooted in background features of the experimental scenario itself (which do not vary across treatment conditions), it is less likely to affect the central quantities of interest experimenters care about. In contrast, the incongruity in treatment inconsistency specifically arises from randomization, and is thus present in some treatment conditions but not in others. As a result, treatment inconsistency is likely to have more pernicious consequences for experimenters, because it manifests itself in the estimates of average treatment effects, which is the quantity of interest experimenters care about directly.[22]

To make the distinction between schema and treatment inconsistency more concrete, we begin with a pretest for our DEMOCRATIC PEACE and NUCLEAR WEAPONS experiments, described in detail in Section 3. Since schema consistency is ultimately an empirical question – which countries do respondents perceive as more or less plausible given the nature of the scenario? – we fielded a pilot study on a sample of about 600 American adults recruited on Amazon Mechanical Turk, in which we described each experimental scenarios in an unnamed country format.[23] We then presented the studies' main outcome questions, and asked respondents to rate the likelihood that each of eleven different countries (Bolivia, Ecuador, Egypt, Ethiopia, Kyrgyzstan, Iran, Malaysia, Sudan, Syria, Turkey, and Vietnam) would be the actor in each scenario. After completing each scenario respondents were presented with a matrix of the eleven countries, and asked: "On a scale of 1–5, where 1 is very unlikely and 5 is very likely, how likely is it that the above scenario describes the following countries?"

Figure 6 depicts respondents' average rating for each of the eleven countries, with 95 percent bootstrapped confidence intervals; the results for the DEMOCRATIC PEACE vignette is shown in panel (a), and the results for the NUCLEAR WEAPONS vignette is shown in panel (b). In each panel, we present the results separately for each study-level treatment (in the DEMOCRATIC PEACE experiment, whether the target is a democracy or not; in the NUCLEAR WEAPONS

---

[22] To put it differently, schema inconsistency has the risk of affecting the intercept, but not the slope coefficient for the treatment effect.

[23] For other work that uses pretests to identify the most reasonable actor for a given scenario, see for example, Chong and Druckman (2007). We randomized the sequencing of scenarios to avoid ordering effects. In addition, since both experiments relate to foreign policy and nuclear weapons, following the first scenario we emphasized that the second scenario describes a different situation.

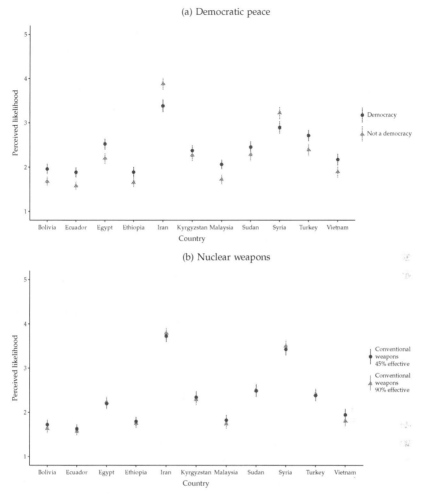

Figure 6 Respondents perceive some countries as more likely candidates than others

Figure 6 shows variation in schema consistency: respondents perceive some countries (like Iran and Syria) to be significantly more likely to be the contexts in which the DEMOCRATIC PEACE and NUCLEAR WEAPONS experiments take place. The top panel, however, also shows evidence of treatment inconsistency: how well respondents perceive certain countries to fit with the experimental scenario depends on the treatment condition. In particular, respondents are significantly less likely to situate the scenario in Iran if the country is described as a democracy than if the country is described as nondemocratic.

experiment, whether conventional weapons would be 90 percent effective, or 45 percent effective).

Both panels of Figure 6 show considerable variation in schema inconsistency across candidate countries, as respondents perceive some countries to be much better fits for the experimental scenario than others. In particular, Iran and Syria are seen by respondents as the most likely countries for the scenario, while Ecuador and Bolivia are seen as the least likely countries to "fit" the scenario. Yet, the two panels differ from one another in an important way: in the NUCLEAR WEAPONS experiment, the perceived likelihood of the vignette taking place in any given country does not vary with the treatment conditions, but in the DEMOCRATIC PEACE experiment, the likelihood assessments are a function of the experimental condition. In particular, respondents see the scenario as much less likely to take place in Iran when the country is described as democratic than when the country is described as nondemocratic ($p<0.01$). We also observe effects in the other direction for other countries (e.g., the scenario is seen as more likely to take place in Malaysia if the country is described as democratic than nondemocratic – $p<0.01$), though the effect sizes are smaller. We also observe that there are often tradeoffs between schema and treatment inconsistency: for example, the regime type treatment affects Kyrgyzstan the least (perhaps because respondents had the weakest priors about that country's regime type), but Kyrgyzstan is also seen as significantly less schema consistent than Iran or Syria are, for example ($p<0.01$).

The question, though, is what effect schema and treatment consistency have on the results experimenters obtain in their studies. We therefore used these pretest results to motivate the design of our DEMOCRATIC PEACE and NUCLEAR WEAPONS experiments, where we randomized the identity of the actors presented to respondents. In both experiments, a quarter of respondents were presented our baseline condition, where the target country was left unnamed, and a quarter of respondents were presented a fictional country (Malaguay). The remaining respondents were assigned either schema consistent or schema inconsistent countries, as determined by our pretest. In the NUCLEAR WEAPONS experiment, the schema consistent country was Syria, and the schema inconsistent country was Bolivia. In both iterations of the DEMOCRATIC PEACE experiment, the schema inconsistent country was Ecuador, and the schema consistent countries were either Iran (which is schema consistent but treatment inconsistent) and Turkey (which the pretest suggested was relatively schema consistent, but significantly less treatment inconsistent than Iran was ($p<0.05$)).

Comparing across studies therefore allows us to decouple schema consistency from treatment consistency. If our estimates of the study-level treatment effects do not significantly differ regardless of which of the five countries are used in the experiments, this suggests experimentalists may have little reason to worry about either schema or treatment inconsistency. If the results differ between Bolivia and Syria in the NUCLEAR WEAPONS experiment, or Turkey and

Ecuador in the DEMOCRATIC PEACE experiment, this suggests schema inconsistency has the potential to distort our experimental findings. If the results differ between Iran and Turkey in the DEMOCRATIC PEACE experiment, however, this suggests we should be concerned about treatment inconsistency.

To test the effect of actor identities, we therefore interact our country-name treatment with each study's original treatment, and present results for both our DEMOCRATIC PEACE studies and the NUCLEAR WEAPONS study in Figure 7 (Panel (a) and (b) respectively). In these figures, our main quantity of interest is the interaction between the original treatment and our additional country identity treatment.[24]

As demonstrated in Figure 7, most country-name conditions do not seem to moderate the main treatment effects. Results obtained from fictional countries do not significantly differ from results from unnamed countries.[25] Schema consistency also appears to display relatively little effect: neither Syria nor Bolivia nor Ecuador nor Turkey significantly moderate the study-level treatment effects.[26] The notable exception is for Iran in both of the DEMOCRATIC PEACE experiments, where there are significant interaction terms between the democracy treatment and the Iran treatment.[27]

As shown in the top panel of Figure 7, we find that using Iran as a country name (schema consistent, but treatment inconsistent) in the DEMOCRATIC PEACE experiment significantly attenuates each study's average treatment effects (i.e., the effect of an adversary's regime type on respondents' support for attacking the adversary). We show in Table 5 that respondents are less likely to accept the democracy treatment for Iran, and in Section 7 we find that respondents who are high in political knowledge – who are most likely to know Iran is not a democracy – are primarily responsible for the differential effect for Iran. In substantive terms, we find that for respondents exposed to the Iran country condition, the average treatment effect of the study's original democracy treatment is indistinguishable from zero.[28] Notably, this pattern does not occur for respondents in the Turkey condition (which is significantly less treatment inconsistent and in which the average treatment effect (ATE) is significant at $p<0.05$), and the interaction term between the Turkey treatment and the

---

[24] In all the figures that follow in this section, point estimates are shown with 95 percent confidence intervals, and all outcomes are standardized for ease of comparability

[25] p value for difference between made up and unnamed country: DEMOCRATIC PEACE I=0.547, NUCLEAR WEAPONS=.346.

[26] p values for difference between country name and no name condition for Syria ($p=0.760$), Bolivia ($p=.375$), Ecuador ($p=.326$), Turkey ($p=.253$).

[27] DEMOCRATIC PEACE I: $p<0.01$ and II: $p<0.01$.

[28] p values for ATE in Iran condition: DEMOCRATIC PEACE I=.633 and II=.708.

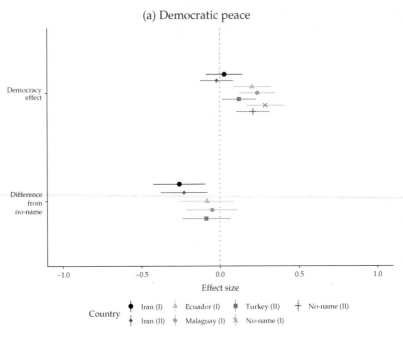

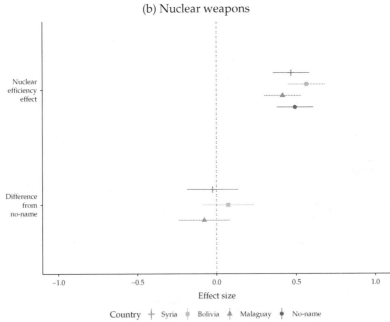

Figure 7 Limited moderating effects of country identity

Figure 7 shows that manipulating the country identity does not significantly moderate treatment effects in the NUCLEAR WEAPONS experiment, but can mute treatment effects in the DEMOCRATIC PEACE experiment when a highly treatment inconsistent country is selected (i.e., Iran).

democracy treatment is not statistically significant (*p*=.253). The fact that Turkey and Ecuador display a similar pattern of results (even though the former is schema consistent and the latter is not) but Turkey and Iran do not (even though both are schema consistent) suggests that experimenters should be particularly concerned about treatment consistency, but less so about schema consistency.

5.2 Salience of Political Candidates

We now examine whether, and how, the level of abstraction matters when the actor in an experiment is a politician. When conducting experiments on politicians, researchers must first evaluate whether there are ethical considerations that would prevent them from using certain types of actors. For example, it may be inappropriate to use real politicians in an experiment if doing so could harm the reputation of the politician, such as by presenting respondents with a false news story about the individual's background. On the other hand, there are many times when researchers have more degrees of freedom to select from hypothetical or real-world actors. McDonald, Croco, and Turitto (2019) offer one important example, experimentally testing whether policy reversals by former President Trump are punished by the public. By contrast, many scholars opt for hypothetical actors, as is common in candidate evaluation experiments in American and comparative politics. While scholars have begun to probe the consequences of these design choices, it remains unclear how and when levels of abstraction matter when using politicians in experimental designs.

To test the effects of using real versus fake politicians in experiments, we turn to our ELITE CUES experiment. The experiment randomized whether an out-party endorsement was by a made-up politician (Stephen Smith [D or R], our pooled baseline condition), a low salience politician (Senators Mike Rounds [R] or Tom Carper [D]), or a high salience politician (Donald Trump [R] or Joe Biden [D]).

Similar to our analysis of the effects of country names, we interact our actor identity treatments with each study's original treatment, and present results in Figure 8. In this figure, our main quantity of interest is the interaction between the original treatment and our additional actor identity treatment.

As demonstrated in Figure 8, there is no difference between using the fictional actor (baseline condition) and the low-salience real actors. However, we do find that using high-salience actors amplifies the endorsement treatment effects (when compared to baseline made-up actors). The difference in effects between the low- and high-salience actors in the ELITE CUES experiment

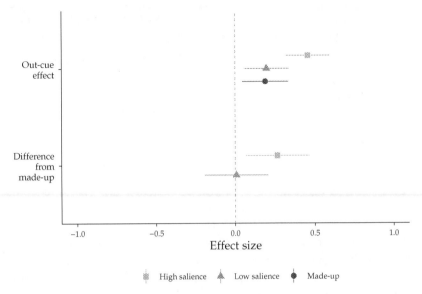

Figure 8 Some moderating effects of politician identity

Figure 8 finds some evidence that employing real-world high-salient actors can moderate average treatment effects.

highlights that there are times when actor selection may be quite consequential. In this study, the increase in opposition resulting from receiving an out-group cue remains regardless of whether the actor is low or high salience, but the magnitude of the effect is significantly larger when the actor is highly salient ($p<0.05$).

There are two groups of potential mechanisms to explain the actor identity results from the ELITE CUES experiment. The first is a standard online processing model (Hastie and Park, 1986) in which respondents keep a running tally of evaluations that are updated when they come into contact with new information. McDonald (2020) proposes a version of this argument, arguing that hypothetical actors (compared to real actors) magnify treatment effects (by decreasing the role of prior knowledge or beliefs), and increase the cognitive burden on respondents, which would show up in increased response latency and lowered treatment recall (again, compared to real politicians). A related mechanism that might be operative in this model is differential treatment recall, in which respondents are better able to recall treatments from salient actors than nonsalient ones, who they simply overlook.

To assess the predictions, we employ a similar test as McDonald (2020) and examine whether the type of actor is associated with greater response latency. As shown in Figure 9, we do not find that there is a significant effect of the actor identity treatment on response latency in our ELITE CUES experiment,

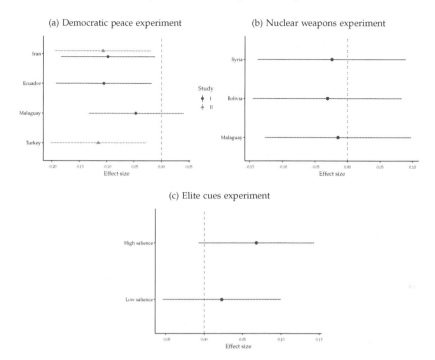

Figure 9 Effects of actor identity on response latency

Figure 9 shows the effect of actor identity treatments on response latency. In all Figures, In the Democratic Peace and Nuclear Weapons experiments, the reference category is an unnamed country. In the Elite Cues experiment, the reference category is a made up politician.

or in the NUCLEAR WEAPONS experiment.[29] In the two DEMOCRATIC PEACE experiments, we do find that respondents presented with real countries display a shorter response time than those given an unnamed country,[30] but crucially, respondents given real countries do not display significantly different response latencies than those presented with fictional countries ($p=0.14$). In general, then, if we think of response latency as a proxy for cognitive burden, these results do not suggest that the choice between real versus fictional countries, or salient versus fictional politicians, significantly affects the cognitive burden experienced by respondents, though named versus unnamed countries can make a difference.

---

[29] p values for ELITE CUES: Low salience ($p=.561$) and high salience ($p=0.077$). NUCLEAR WEAPONS p values for country-name conditions: Malaguay ($p=.797$), Bolivia ($p=.596$), Syria ($p=.675$).

[30] Iran in both studies, Ecuador, and Turkey are all significantly different than unnamed conditions at $p<.05$.

A second potential mechanism that could be at work here is differential treatment recall, in which respondents are better able to recall treatments from salient or real-world actors than nonsalient ones. Importantly, we do not find systematic evidence that respondents are more likely to correctly recall the treatment condition when given more salient actors.[31] We do find, however, that actor identity can interact with the treatment condition in ways that affects treatment recall, as Table 5 shows. In particular, in the DEMOCRATIC PEACE experiments, we find that respondents in the Iran condition are significantly less likely to correctly recall the regime type treatment when assigned to the democracy condition.[32] In other words, our treatment recall data illustrate the challenge of treatment inconsistency: one reason why the effect of the study-level treatment shrinks when the scenario is set in Iran is because respondents have prior beliefs about Iran's regime type, meaning they are either more likely to ignore or refuse to accept the regime type treatment when in the democracy condition. Most importantly, we do not observe similar patterns in the NUCLEAR WEAPONS and ELITE CUES experiments, where the study-level treatments largely do not interact with the actor identity conditions.[33]

One additional interpretation of our results in the ELITE CUES experiment has to do with simple Bayesian models of persuasion. Bayesian models would first predict that when the outcome variable measures *attitudes toward a policy*, stronger respondent priors about the policy's endorser should lead to *more* updating. Our finding in ELITE CUES are consistent with this finding. An additional prediction from this same Bayesian model – untested in our study – would be that when the outcome variable measures *attitudes about an actor*, stronger respondent priors should lead to *less* updating in response to information about the actor, consistent with Croco, Hanmer, and McDonald (2021). In this sense, because respondents are likely to have stronger attitudes about more salient real-world actors than less salient ones, differences between real and hypothetical actors should be smaller for less salient actors than more salient ones: consistent with the results of Section 4, it is the salience of an actor that matters for questions of experimental design, rather than whether the actor is real or fictional.

---

[31] ELITE CUES $p=0.180$.

[32] p value for effect of Iran on treatment recall: DEMOCRATIC PEACE I $p<0.05$ and II $p<.1$

[33] The exception is the high-salience condition in ELITE CUES, which is marginally significant p values for NUCLEAR WEAPONS: Syria ($p=.526$), Bolivia ($p=.539$), Malaguay ($p=.605$). For ELITE CUES: low salience ($p=0.561$), high salience ($p=.077$).

Table 5 Rate of treatment recall by actor identity and treatment condition

DEMOCRATIC PEACE I	**Country**	**Not a democracy**	**Democracy**	**Difference**
	No-Name	0.803	0.699	−0.105*
	Iran	0.825	0.589	−0.236*
	Ecuador	0.726	0.748	0.022
	Malaguay	0.834	0.677	−0.157*
DEMOCRATIC PEACE II	Country	Not a democracy	Democracy	Difference
	No-Name	0.725	0.734	0.009
	Iran	0.756	0.636	−0.120*
	Turkey	0.662	0.734	0.072*
NUCLEAR WEAPONS	Country	Not effective	Effective	Difference
	No-Name	0.580	0.602	0.023
	Malaguay	0.553	0.604	0.051
	Bolivia	0.555	0.600	0.045
	Syria	0.596	0.559	−0.037
ELITE CUES	Actor type	In cue	Out cue	Difference
	Made up	0.640	0.585	−0.055
	Low salience	0.619	0.589	−0.030
	High salience	0.636	0.621	−0.016

Note: $^*p<0.05$ in two-proportion Z test

5.3 Conclusion

In this section, we used five experimental studies to explore the consequences of manipulating actor identities in experimental designs. We have three key findings.

First, across three experiments, we found relatively little evidence that schema inconsistency affects the results experimenters obtain. It thus appears that experimenters should not necessarily be concerned that respondents will fail to take studies seriously when the experimental scenario is situated in unlikely contexts. At the same time, however, it is not the case that setting scenarios in unnamed or artificial contexts causes respondents to shed the trappings of the real world altogether: respondents in the NUCLEAR WEAPONS experiment, for example, responded identically when the scenario was set in the fictional country of Malaguay as when it was set in Syria.

Second, more important than schema inconsistency appears to be treatment inconsistency, which occurs when experimenters try to manipulate the characteristics of real-world actors, about which respondents have stronger prior beliefs. Experimenters should therefore be cautious about choosing real-world actors for experimental designs when the purpose of the experiment is to manipulate enduring characteristics of the actors themselves. In the DEMOCRATIC PEACE experiments, for example, respondents who were told that Iran was a democracy were more likely to ignore or set aside the democracy condition, reducing the magnitude of the treatment effect. As we discuss in Section 7, these effects are typically largest among politically sophisticated respondents, who are more likely to recognize treatment inconsistency in the first place. Pretests and/or focus groups can be useful to experimenters in helping them select the actors that make the most sense for the questions they are trying to study.

Third, with regard to experiments about individual politicians, like those often found in American politics experiments, the key distinction is not whether the politician in a study is real or fake, but between high-salience politicians and everyone else. Because respondents have stronger prior beliefs about more salient political candidates, this means that endorsements from more salient candidates will have stronger effects than endorsements from less salient or fictional ones. Conversely, if attitudes toward a political candidate constitute the outcome measure, treatment effects should be weaker on evaluations of salient candidates (respondents' views of which are likely harder to move) than less salient ones.

Because we centered our discussion of actor identity on questions relating to schema inconsistency, treatment inconsistency, and actor salience, there are a number of challenges that this section sidesteps. For example, we do not examine questions of actor identity in correspondence audit experiments, which often seek to study questions of discrimination in an indirect manner by manipulating the names of fictional individuals to proxy for their race and gender (e.g., Bertrand and Mullainathan, 2004; Butler, Nickerson, et al., 2011; White, Nathan, and Faller, 2015). The challenge here is that names contain multiple pieces of information, meaning varying names can inadvertently vary respondents' beliefs about other attributes as well, such as the individual's socioeconomic status (Gaddis, 2017; Landgrave and Weller, 2022). We also do not investigate the consequences of intersectional stereotyping on actor identity choices in experiments: Petsko and Bodenhausen (2019), for example, show that manipulating a target's race also changes respondents' beliefs about the target's sexual orientation. Together, this suggests that manipulating attributes of fake actors can often be no less challenging than attending to questions of treatment consistency when manipulating attributes of real actors.

Although the experiments we field here are all conventional factorial or one-way experimental designs, we believe the same implications here matter for a broader class of experiments as well. One challenge that scholars design-ing conjoint experiments, for example, often face concerns how to handle implausible combinations of attributes, which scholars typically address either by ensuring that all combinations of their treatments are valid (e.g., Dill and Schubiger, 2021) or by imposing randomization constraints (e.g., Hainmueller and Hopkins, 2015, 535, Clary and Siddiqui, 2021). In their study of how observers assess resolve in foreign policy disputes, for example, Kertzer, Ren-shon, and Yarhi-Milo (2021, 316) impose a randomization restriction such that when one of the countries in the dispute is the United States, it is always described as having a powerful military and being a democracy (rather than randomizing military capabilities and regime type independently of the identity of the belligerent). Although not formally couched in terms of treatment incon-sistency, the same logic applies: when respondents have strong priors about the characteristics of real-world actors, presenting combinations of treatments that contradict those priors will weaken the treatment effects.

6 Contextual Detail

When designing experiments, researchers must decide how much contextual detail to include. On one hand, some scholars prefer highly stylized experi-ments left deliberately devoid of detailed context, even if this may come at the expense of ecological validity and mundane realism (Morton and Williams, 2010, 313–14). Such experiments are frequently employed by economists and those testing the implications of formal theory in behavioral experiments (e.g., Dickson, 2009; Dawes, Loewen, and Fowler, 2011; Kanthak and Woon, 2015; Kertzer and Rathbun, 2015; LeVeck and Narang, 2017; Hundley, 2020), but can be found in survey experimental work in political science as well (e.g., Renshon, 2015; Mutz and Kim, 2017; Brutger and Guisinger, 2021; Brutger, 2021). Another tradition originating in psychology regularly employs rich and detailed vignette-based experiments. Such experiments have also been adopted by political scientists (e.g., Rousseau and Garcia-Retamero, 2007; Brooks and Valentino, 2011; Druckman, Peterson, and Slothuus, 2013; Teele, Kalla, and Rosenbluth, 2018; Reeves and Rogowski, 2018; Bracic and Murdie, 2020; Tomz, Weeks, and Yarhi-Milo, 2020; Brutger and Strezhnev, 2022), often with the argument that rich and detailed stimuli more closely resemble the manner in which people would encounter "treatments" in the "real world."

The argument usually offered in favor of contextual detail is that it increases realism and respondent engagement. Yet, apart from Kreps and Roblin (2019) and Bansak and colleagues (2021), there has been little empirical work adjudicating what the consequences of providing richer or sparser stimuli might be. We argue that contextual detail can be thought of as consisting of at least three interrelated dimensions. The first is simply the volume of information provided. The second concerns *how* the information is presented, and here there have been examples of any number of treatment formats in experiments, from bullet-pointed vignettes (Tomz, 2007), to mock news reports (Druckman and Nelson, 2003; Valentino, Neuner, and Vandenbroek, 2018). The third is the content of the information itself, which is orthogonal to its volume. Borrowing from Bansak and colleagues (2021), we make a distinction between two types of additional context: "filler" context – peripheral information that increases the volume of text, but which is not expected to interact with the treatment – and "charged" context that similarly increases the length of the stimulus, but which is more likely to affect how respondents react to the treatment.

In this section, we focus on assessing how the volume of information and the content of the information that comprise contextual detail affect experimental results.[34] We expect that increasing the amount of contextual detail in an experiment will effectively reduce the treatment dosage and therefore reduce the magnitude of identified effects, but also expect the effect of additional context to depend on the context.

Of course, just as is the case with placebo conditions (Porter and Velez, 2022), determining in advance what is "filler" versus "charged" context is not always obvious. One might expect that adding certain additional details, such as the partisanship of the actors, is likely to be charged, since it provides salient information to respondents. However, determining whether other types of contextual detail are charged or not may require specific knowledge of the nature and setting of the study. Researchers may also find it helpful to use focus groups or pretests to assess whether the context they plan to include in their study is "charged" or "filler." In both cases, increasing the amount of contextual detail in an experiment may decrease treatment dosage, and therefore reduce the magnitude of identified effects, but the effect should be larger for charged context than filler context.

---

[34] We direct readers to Kreps and Roblin (2019) for an experimental evaluation of the related question of treatment formats.

6.1 Adding and Subtracting Contextual Detail

To test how contextual detail affects survey responses, our NUCLEAR WEAPONS and IN-GROUP FAVORITISM experiments randomized the contextual detail presented to respondents. We administered two versions of our context treatments. In the NUCLEAR WEAPONS experiment, respondents were either exposed to a reduced context vignette (baseline) or the original elaborate context vignette. In the IN-GROUP FAVORITISM experiment, respondents were either exposed to the original minimal context vignette (baseline), or an extended context vignette which included "filler" or "charged" additional context. In all cases, the extended context vignettes are about 200–250 words longer than the reduced context vignettes. The results from these experiments are displayed in Figure 10. By focusing on the interaction effect of the experiments' original treatments with contextual treatments, both panels of Figure 10 lend insight into the consequences of providing additional context in experimental vignettes.

As demonstrated in panel (a) of Figure 10, exposing respondents to the original rich experimental vignette in the NUCLEAR WEAPONS experiment has a negative moderating effect on the study's main treatment ($p<0.01$).[35] Put differently, the extended experimental vignette dampens the effect of the NUCLEAR WEAPONS experiment's substantive treatment (nuclear effectiveness). While this dampening would lead scholars to estimate more conservative treatment effects, we find no evidence that it would lead scholars to draw opposite inferences from their studies, though they may be more likely to find a null effect.

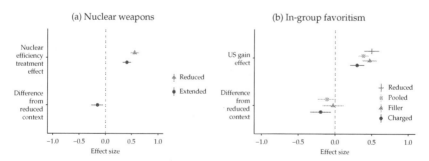

Figure 10 Adding contextual detail attenuates treatment effects

Figure 10 shows that increased contextual detail weakens substantive treatment effects in the NUCLEAR WEAPONS and IN-GROUP FAVORITISM experiments.

---

[35] In all the figures in this section, point estimates are shown with 95 percent confidence intervals, and all outcomes are standardized for ease of comparability.

Panel (b) of Figure 10 provides us with further insight in to the moderating effects of contextual detail. In this panel, we consider the general effect of adding contextual detail to experimental vignettes (green square – pooled model), as well as the particular effects of adding either "filler" or "charged" context. Results from panel (b) further suggest that adding contextual detail to experimental vignettes dampens treatment effects. Indeed, the moderating effect of extended contextual detail (compared to a baseline minimal-context condition) – when pooling together both "filler" and "charged" context conditions – is marginally significant ($p<0.08$). Clearly, as evident in panel (b) of Figure 10 this effect is driven by the "charged" context condition, which in and of itself has a statistically significant impact on the size (but not direction) of main treatment effects.

6.2 Treatment Recall and Response Latency

To better understand why adding contextual detail to experimental vignettes dampens the experiments original treatment effects, we consider the effects of our contextual detail treatment on treatment recall success. To do so, we regress respondents' recall success of the original study-level treatments (nuclear effectiveness and the expected consequences of trade) on respondents' contextual detail condition. Figure 11 demonstrates that increased context in experimental design hinders respondents' ability to successfully recall the treatment condition to which they were assigned.[36] This finding is consistent with the idea that adding more context effectively "waters down" the treatment, given that the proportion of the vignette that is composed of the treatment declines as additional context is added.

We also evaluate whether adding additional context affects the cognitive burden of the task for respondents, which we measure using response latency: the length of time it takes subjects to submit their response (Lenzner, Kaczmirek, and Lenzner, 2010). As we show in Figure 12, there is strong evidence that longer vignettes increase cognitive burden measured by response latency ($p<0.01$ for all point estimates). This is not particularly surprising, given that it should take respondents longer to read the additional text, but it does provide further credence to the notion that increasing the volume of information that respondents are being presented with increases the demands on the respondent, which likely contributes to lower levels of treatment recall and smaller average treatment effects.

---

[36] p value for charged context ($p<0.01$), for filler context ($p<0.01$), for extended context ($p<0.05$).

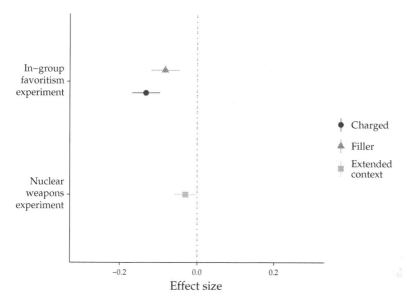

Figure 11 Contextual detail reduces treatment recall

Figure 11 indicates that adding contextual detail reduces the the likelihood of accurate treatment recall in the NUCLEAR WEAPONS and IN-GROUP FAVORITISM experiments.

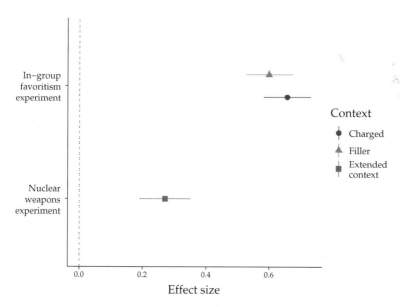

Figure 12 Contextual detail increases response time

Figure 12 demonstrates how increasing context in experimental vignettes increases cognitive burden of respondents (measured by response time for the main outcome variable) in the NUCLEAR WEAPONS and IN-GROUP FAVORITISM experiments.

6.3 Conclusion

The results from our tests of contextual detail are quite consistent across studies. We find that additional context leads to more conservative estimates of treatment effects, dampening treatment effects by hindering respondents' ability to successfully recall the main treatment. This suggests that experimentalists face a choice when deciding how much, and what type, of context they will include in their experimental designs. Choosing the appropriate level of contextual detail in experimental work thus depends on how much statistical power the researcher has, as well as the purpose of the study. If the purpose is to demonstrate that an effect exists, a sparser experimental design better enables researchers to identify this effect, but if the purpose is instead to understand how important an effect might be relative to other considerations, or whether respondents in a more naturalistic setting would be likely to receive the treatment (Barabas and Jerit, 2010), a more contextually rich design may be beneficial, since it better mirrors the real-world information environment. Experimentalists should thus be guided by their theoretical quantity of interest and an assessment of power of their study when deciding whether to employ a contextually rich or sparse experimental design.

This decision of how to design one's study is also complicated by the fact that the type of additional context matters, with charged context having a greater dampening effect on treatment effects than filler content. Of course, evaluating what type of context is charged versus filler is a challenging process, which is likely to vary based on the nature and setting of the study. We encourage researchers to critically assess whether the contextual detail they are adding is likely to be charged, which will often require specific knowledge of the topic of interest, and potentially the subject pool as well. When in doubt, experimentalists may use pretests or focus groups to evaluate how respondents interpret additional context, which can help determine whether the additional context is charged or not, and the appropriate design for the researchers' question of interest.

7 Individual Differences and Heterogeneous Treatment Effects

Thus far we have focused on how varying levels of abstraction and detail may alter the main effects of researchers' experiments. However, there are at least two reasons one might also be interested in testing whether the effects of abstraction and detail vary across different types of respondents.

The first concerns testing theoretical microfoundations (Kertzer, 2017). The effects of treatment inconsistency in the context of actor identity discussed in Section 5, for example, rested on assumptions that respondents have prior knowledge about real-world actors (such as the regime type of real countries, or the partisan preferences of real politicians); if this is the case, we should expect that higher knowledge respondents would be more likely to be aware of treatment inconsistency than less politically sophisticated respondents. Testing whether we in fact detect heterogeneous treatment effects along these dimensions therefore bolsters our understanding of why these treatments work, which also influences how we design our studies in the first place.

The second concerns questions about sampling. Experiments are often fielded on a wide range of samples: convenience samples of college students and community members, online survey panels of diverse national samples targeted to match various population parameters, nationally representative samples, and so on. While knife-edge distinctions between convenience versus probability-based sampling are increasingly murky (in an era of single-digit response rates, most "probability-based" samples now require significant model-based adjustments), experimenters are often interested in how potentially idiosyncratic characteristics of their sample have implications for their results (Druckman and Kam, 2011; Berinsky, Huber, and Lenz, 2012; Chandler, Mueller, and Paolacci, 2014; Mullinix et al., 2015; Coppock and McClellan, 2019; Lupton, 2019; Kertzer, 2020), which requires gaining a more solid understanding of their sample's idiosyncracies in the first place (Huff and Tingley, 2015). Crucially, the use of nonprobability samples should not bias the average treatment effects recovered in an experiment as long as the characteristics on which a sample differs do not interact with the treatment. If it is the case that more politically sophisticated respondents respond systematically differently to abstraction or detail in experimental design, researchers planning on fielding experiments on a high-knowledge sample face steeper tradeoffs they should keep in mind than researchers fielding experiments on a less politically sophisticated respondents.

In the discussion in this section, we first begin with our theoretical expectations, focusing on four respondent-level differences (political knowledge, need for cognition, strength of partisanship, and strength of affect toward countries) that have the potential to interact with some of our three dimensions of abstraction in experimental design, although as we note, we do not expect each of these features to interact with all three dimensions. We then present our findings. We find relatively strong evidence for the effects of political knowledge – helping shore up our understanding of the microfoundations of our experimental results in Section 5 – but weaker evidence for the effects of the other individual differences.

7.1 Theoretical Expectations

Although there is no shortage of individual differences researchers could turn to when testing for heterogeneous treatment effects by respondent type, to keep the discussion in this section tractable, we focus on four characteristics of interest. These were chosen either because they directly implicate micro-foundations for the theoretical mechanisms posited in the previous sections or have implications for questions of survey sampling.

Political Knowledge

The first individual difference we look at is *political knowledge*: do people who know more about politics respond significantly differently to abstraction and detail in survey experiments? Political knowledge is an important potential moderator to examine for a number of reasons. First, public opinion polls frequently show that ordinary citizens (especially in the United States) tend to be relatively uninformed about politics. Even at the height of the COVID-19 pandemic, for example, Pew found that a third of Americans were unaware of who Anthony Fauci was, and two-thirds were unaware of the size of the pandemic economic aid bill passed by Congress in March 2020.[37] Second, a voluminous body of evidence shows that citizens who are more knowledgeable about politics display systematic differences in their political attitudes and behavior from those who are less knowledgeable (e.g., Fiske, Lau, and Smith, 1990; Delli Carpini and Keeter, 1996; Althaus, 1998). In spite of this, survey experiments in political science often ask respondents to think through relatively complex political phenomena, about which respondents may have relatively little prior knowledge or background information. What implications does this have for the results our experiments obtain?

While we have no prior theoretical expectation that political knowledge should moderate the effects of situational hypotheticality or contextual detail, we do expect it to have important implications for questions of actor identity. This should manifest itself in two forms in particular. One of the striking findings from Section 5 was that experimenters should be wary of treatment inconsistency: cases where experiments randomize features of real-world actors, and in which not all the levels of the treatments being assigned correspond to respondents' prior beliefs about the actors. For example: if Americans think of Iran as nondemocratic, respondents presented with a foreign policy scenario featuring a democratic Iran are less likely to accept the treatment. If the effect of treatment inconsistency hinges on respondents having prior beliefs

---

[37] See www.pewresearch.org/pathways-2020/.

about these real-world actors, we should expect these effects to be larger for more politically knowledgeable respondents.

Another striking finding from Section 5 was that using salient actors can increase the size of treatment effects in endorsement experiments. Since the mechanism here also hinges on salient actors mattering because respondents are more likely to have prior beliefs about salient actors than less salient ones, we would expect that this effect would be more pronounced among high-knowledge respondents than low-knowledge ones.

To test for the moderating effects of political knowledge, in our Nuclear Weapons and In-Group Favoritism experiments, we measured political knowledge with two multiple choice questions regarding: (1) the identity of the United Kingdom's current prime minister, and (2) the length of US House of Representative terms for office. In the Elite Cues experiment, we added a third question regarding the identity of Israel's current prime minister. An exploration of our knowledge scale suggests that there is a noticeable degree of variation in political knowledge among respondents. Respondents in the first two experiments successfully answered approximately one out of two questions correctly ($\mu=1.1$ and $\sigma^2=0.7$), and in the third experiment successfully answered close to two out of three questions correctly ($\mu=1.7$ and $\sigma^2=0.9$). To facilitate ease of interpretation, we split our sample in two based on whether or not respondents scored above the mean level of political knowledge.

Need for Cognition

The second characteristic we explore is need for cognition (NFC) (Cacioppo and Petty, 1982): the extent to which people vary in epistemic motivation, or how much they like to think things through. We do not expect NFC to moderate the impact of situational hypotheticality or actor identity, but we do consider the possibility that NFC moderates the effects of contextual detail. One of our findings from Section 6 was that contextual detail attenuates treatment effects, which we suggested was due to this additional information crowding out the treatment. One possibility is that these crowding out effects are more pronounced among low-cognition respondents than high-cognition ones, who may be more attentive.

To test for the moderating effects of NFC, we utilized a shorter-form version of the NFC scale based on fourteen commonly used questions (Cacioppo and Petty, 1982; Rathbun, Kertzer, and Paradis, 2017). As with political knowledge, for ease of interpretation we mean-split this index to create two subsamples of respondents, based on whether they display high (above average) or low (below average) levels of NFC. We only included the NFC items in the dispositional battery that accompanied the IN-GROUP FAVORITISM, NUCLEAR WEAPONS, and DEMOCRATIC PEACE I experiments, so we limit our analysis of NFC to those three experiments.

Strength of Partisanship and Affect toward Countries

In our experiments, we featured two types of actors that are frequently used in political science experiments: politicians (frequently used in experiments in American and comparative politics) and countries (frequently used in experiments in international relations). Two theoretically relevant individual differences that might arise in experiments featuring real versions of these two types of actors are respondents' strength of partisanship, and their strength of affect toward the countries in question, respectively. If political knowledge matters *cognitively*, because higher knowledge respondents have stronger beliefs about these actors (for example, about the policy positions of the political figures, or the characteristics of the countries), these other two characteristics are relevant *affectively*, because some types of respondents might have stronger feelings toward these actors more generally (Burden and Klofstad, 2005). If partisanship is a social identity (Mason, 2018), stronger partisans will engage in more intergroup differentiation than weak partisans will, and will be more responsive to real salient political candidates. Similarly, individuals who report feeling very warm or very cold attitudes toward specific real-world countries (Herrmann, 2013) should be more sensitive to the choice of real countries than individuals who have relatively neutral attitudes toward specific countries. As with the case of political knowledge, then, our theoretical expectations for strength of partisanship and affect toward countries manifest themselves in regard to the actor identity dimension, rather than situational hypotheticality or contextual detail.

We measured respondents' strength of partisanship in the ELITE CUES experiment, and respondents' affect toward countries as part of our second DEMOCRATIC PEACE experiment. To measure partisan strength, we asked Democratic (Republican) respondents whether they identify as "strong" or "not very strong" Democrats (Republicans). We classify Democratic and Republican respondents who identify as strong partisans (not very strong), as respondents with "Strong PID" ("Weak PID").[38]

To measure the strength of respondents' affect toward countries, we presented all respondents with feeling thermometers, asking them to indicate how warmly they feel toward a range of countries on a scale from 0-100, which

---

[38] We follow the original study in excluding leaners from the analysis.

included two countries used as actor identity treatments (Iran and Turkey). We then coded the absolute distance of a respondents' affect toward a given country from the scale midpoint, and subset our sample to differentiate between respondents who reported affect below the median distance (Iran=30, Turkey=15), or greater than or equal to the median distance.

Finally, for all four of these sources of heterogeneity, there is a key limitation that should be kept in mind in the discussion of the results that follow. To preserve ease of interpretability, we dichotomize the moderators (often through mean-splitting). Although this facilitates ease of interpretation and sidesteps presenting cumbersome three-way interactions in the text itself, it also reduces our sample size and power in each analysis, such that we encourage readers to exercise caution when interpreting these additional results.

7.2 Results

Political Knowledge

In the discussion in Section 7.1, we hypothesized that respondents higher in political knowledge will display more sensitivity to treatment inconsistency, since they're more likely to be aware of the incongruous combination in the first place. In Figure 13 we present the results for our NUCLEAR WEAPONS and DEMOCRATIC PEACE experiments. In each row of the figure, we interact the country name treatment with the main substantive treatment, subsetting the results between high- and low-knowledge respondents. As Section 5 discussed, treatment inconsistency is not an issue in the NUCLEAR WEAPONS experiment, since the substantive treatment (the relative efficacy of nuclear strike versus a conventional weapons strike) is orthogonal to the country chosen.

The bottom row of panels shows, however, results that are broadly consistent with our expectations in the DEMOCRATIC PEACE experiments: for the high knowledge respondents, the democracy treatment substantively weakens when a treatment-inconsistent country (Iran) is chosen (compared to unnamed).[39] For low-knowledge respondents – also broadly consistent with our expectations – we find the democracy treatment attenuating the effect of the Iran (treatment-inconsistent) country condition (compared to unnamed), though to a lesser degree.[40] A more formal regression does find support for our expectations: a model with a three-way interaction term confirms that the effect of the Iran treatment on the democracy treatment is significantly more negative as

---

[39] Among high knowledge subjects in DEMOCRATIC PEACE I $p<0.05$ and II $p<0.01$.

[40] That is, we find evidence of the attenuation in DEMOCRATIC PEACE I but not in DEMOCRATIC PEACE II. DEMOCRATIC PEACE I $p<0.05$, and II $p<0.854$.

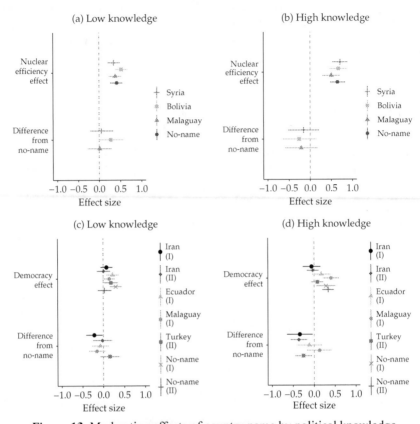

Figure 13 Moderating effects of country name by political knowledge

Figure 13 shows the moderating effects of country name, across different levels of survey respondents' political knowledge in the NUCLEAR WEAPONS experiment (top row) and DEMOCRATIC PEACE experiment (bottom row).

respondents' political knowledge increases ($p<0.033$ in DEMOCRATIC PEACE I, $p<0.026$ in DEMOCRATIC PEACE II). Interestingly, we also find a similar attenuating effect for high-knowledge respondents when manipulating Turkey's regime type ($p<0.003$), even though Turkey was seen as significantly more treatment consistent in our pretest than Iran was. This suggests that for researchers who anticipate conducting studies on high-knowledge respondents in particular (such as on samples of political elites – Kertzer and Renshon, 2022) – choices of actor identity likely have larger consequences than they do for less politically sophisticated samples.

In Figure 14, we continue examining the moderating effects of actor identity across varying levels of political knowledge, this time focusing on the moderating effect of high- and low-salience actors. As a reminder, in our main analysis, we find that employing high-salience actors has a positive

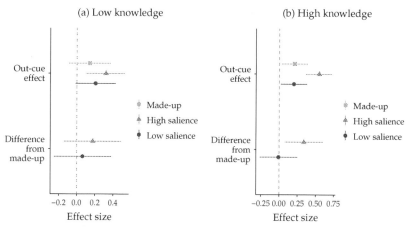

Figure 14 Moderating effects of actor identity by political knowledge

Figure 14 shows the moderating effects of actor identity, across different levels of survey respondents' political knowledge in the ELITE CUES experiment.

moderating effect, increasing the size of the average treatment effects. Consistent with our hypotheses, we find that high-knowledge respondents respond more forcefully to cues from high-salience actors when splitting our samples ($p<0.05$), although here a formal test from a three-way interaction model is not statistically significant ($p=.994$).

Need for Cognition

We next turn to the potential moderating effects of NFC, where we hypothesized that high-cognition respondents would be less sensitive to contextual detail than their low-cognition counterparts in Figure 15. In the IN-GROUP FAVORITISM study we find that contextual detail significantly reduces the size of the substantive treatment effect for low-cognition respondents ($p<0.1$), but not for high-cognition ones ($p=.983$). However, against our hypotheses, the results for the interaction term in a formal three-way interaction model between the substantive treatment, contextual detail, and NFC is not statistically significant ($p=.243$).

In the NUCLEAR WEAPONS experiment, Figure 15 shows that we find that the ATE of nuclear efficiency (the main substantive treatment from the original study) is positive and statistically significant in *both* the extended and reduced context conditions for *both* low- and high-NFC subjects ($p<0.01$). We further find some evidence that adding extended context slightly attenuates ATEs for high-NFC subjects ($p<0.1$), but not for low-NFC subjects ($p=0.27$). Altogether then, we find relatively little evidence in favor of our hypothesized countervailing effect of NFC.

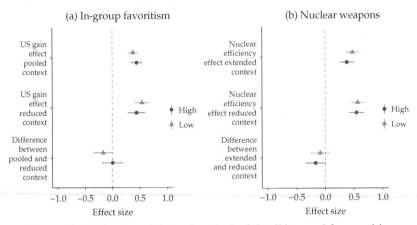

Figure 15 Moderating effects of contextual detail by need for cognition

Figure 15 shows the moderating effects of context, across different levels of survey respondents' need for cognition, in the IN-GROUP FAVORITISM and NUCLEAR WEAPONS experiments.

Strong Partisanship and Affect toward Countries

In Section 7.1 we hypothesized that individuals with more extreme affect toward the actors in question – either because they are strong partisans responding to salient politicians, or individuals with embedded images about specific countries in the experimental scenarios – should be more sensitive to actor identity considerations. Stronger partisans should be more responsive to real salient political candidates, while individuals who report feeling very warm or very cold attitudes toward specific real-world countries should be more sensitive to the choice of real countries.

Figure 16 explores the potential moderating role of strength of partisanship in the ELITE CUES experiment, and finds strikingly similar results across both strong and weak partisans. Figure 17 suggests relatively more support for our strength of affect toward countries hypothesis in the DEMOCRATIC PEACE experiment. Individuals who feel more warmly or coldly toward either Turkey (panel a) or Iran (panel b) display a significant and negative interaction between the substantive treatment and the country name treatment, while respondents who have relatively neutral affect toward each of these countries do not. In both cases, however, the three-way interaction between regime type, country name, and extremity of affect is not statistically significant.[41]

---

[41] *p* value for interaction with Iran condition (*p*=.411) and with Turkey condition (*p*=.361).

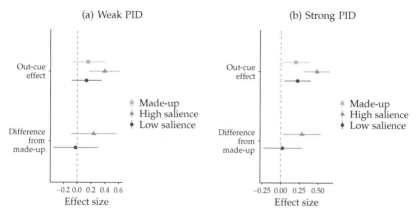

Figure 16 Moderating effects of actor identity by strength of partisanship

Figure 16 shows the moderating effects of actor identity, across different levels of survey respondents' strength of party identification, in the ELITE CUES experiment.

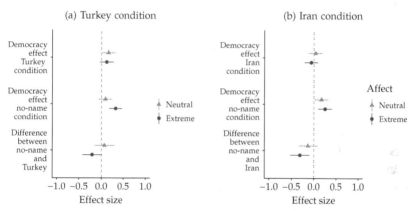

Figure 17 Moderating effects of country name by strength of affect toward countries

Figure 17 shows the moderating effects of country name, across subsamples with neutral and extreme attitudes toward the country in question in the DEMOCRATIC PEACE experiments.

7.3 Conclusion

In this section, we looked at the effects of four theoretically motivated sources of respondent heterogeneity: political knowledge, need for cognition, strength of partisanship, and affect toward countries. We found more evidence in favor of some of our hypotheses than others. In particular, we found our strongest evidence for the exacerbating effects of political knowledge (which enhances the effects of design choices about actor identity), no evidence for the mitigating effects of need for cognition, little evidence in favor of strength of partisanship, and some (but relatively weak) evidence in favor of strength of affect towards countries.[42] The political knowledge results are particularly striking because they suggest that the lack of political knowledge pervasive in mass samples can actually mitigate design tradeoffs associated with abstraction and concrete detail in survey experiments: it is the most politically sophisticated respondents in our studies who recognize treatment inconsistency. The more politically sophisticated that experimenters expect their samples to be (as in samples of political elites, for example), the more they should consider how treatment inconsistency may affect their experimental results.

We focused on these four traits because they shed light on theoretical microfoundations, as well as having potential implications for questions of survey sampling. They are certainly not the only individual differences experimenters might potentially be interested in that bear on calibrating degrees of abstraction in experimental design, and we encourage other researchers to extend our analysis by looking at other theoretically relevant sources of respondent heterogeneity as well.

One such source worth studying involves survey mode and fielding method. It is difficult to field contextually detailed survey experiments over the telephone, for example, which is one reason why the early computer-assisted telephone interview–based survey experiments tended to feature relatively short vignettes compared to those used in laboratory experiments that could show respondents lengthy news reports (Sniderman, 2011). Today, telephone-based surveys tend to be outnumbered by Internet-based ones in political science (particularly for studies fielded in the United States), but experimenters often face decisions about whether to permit respondents to take their studies on their mobile devices versus a personal computer.

In this sense, we can think of mobile device use as less a dispositional trait and more simply a situational characteristic. While mobile use is unlikely to be random – younger respondents are presumably more likely to take studies on mobile devices than older respondents are, for example – it is nonetheless worth studying for our purposes because mobile devices tend to feature smaller screens than laptop or desktop computers do. Certain types of experiments – such as choice-based conjoint experiments (e.g. Hainmueller and Hopkins, 2015; Kertzer, Renshon, and Yarhi-Milo, 2021) – are likely to be particularly illegible on mobile devices, attenuating treatment effects.

---

[42] See Appendix §§4–6 for a battery of additional tests of the moderating effects of these four characteristics.

Due to our own theoretical priors, we precluded respondents from taking our first set of experiments on mobile devices, because they involved larger amounts of contextual detail, and we presumed a smaller screen size would make scrolling through a longer vignette more cumbersome. We are therefore unable to test whether the moderating effects of contextual detail are exacerbated on mobile devices compared to on desktop or laptop computers. We encourage subsequent researchers to test whether the theoretical intuitions that mandated our decision are accurate. We did allow mobile devices for a subset of our respondents in later experiments; in Appendix §7 we show that mobile device use does not seem to affect situational hypotheticality or actor identity, but because we did not manipulate contextual detail in those studies, we are unable to investigate its effects in regard to contextual detail.

8 Conclusion

We began this Element by calling attention to a significant challenge faced by political scientists who seek to test their theories using experimental designs: in most cases, they have a wide degree of latitude in how to design experimental stimuli. They must make choices about whether to use real actor names, make them up, or leave them unnamed, whether to add rich, contextual detail (and if so, how much, and what kind), how to present the information in the experiment (whether explicitly hypothetical, ambiguously hypothetical, or as real), whether to use deception, and so on. In confronting the issues raised by these "design degrees of freedom," scholars have no shortage of folk wisdom to fall back on from their peers, mentors and textbooks, but little in the way of empirically guided, practical advice. Indeed, the "conventional wisdom" on which they can rely is either nonexistent or contradictory. The strong preference from those in the economics tradition is to use sparse, abstract designs, while those in the psychology tradition prefer experimental designs with rich contextual detail, typically using real or made-up actor names (as opposed to unnamed actors). One common theme from both camps is that – whatever the researcher chooses – they will face a tradeoff between experimental control and generalizability. However, despite a recognition that these questions are, ultimately, subject to study and research like many other problems (e.g., Friedman, Friedman, and Sunder, 1994), there is little in the way of theoretical frameworks or empirically minded guidance for researchers who face these issues.

Our contribution here is twofold. First, we provided a conceptual framework that helps to make sense of the many choices that experimentalists face in terms of the degree of abstraction or concreteness of their designs. In so doing, we draw from construal level theory in making a distinction between "primary, defining features, which are relatively stable and invariant, and secondary features, which may change with changes in context and hence are omitted from the higher-level representation" (Shapira et al., 2012, 231). This flexible definition is easily applied to experimental designs, in which abstract representations represent an object's most essential features ("a candidate") while more concrete representations add context and detail and include subordinate considerations ("a female Democratic candidate from the Midwest").

Our framework outlines three dimensions of abstraction – situational hypotheticality, actor identity and contextual detail – and helps us to classify prototypical experiments along these three dimensions. Most importantly, our framework and theoretical discussion help to clarify when there are, and are not, important tradeoffs between experimental control and generalizability. For example, a common concern is that using more abstract designs may lower control since respondents may impute additional features into the experimental scenario. In contrast, we argue that abstraction may in some cases enhance, rather than decrease, experimental control, which, in any case, experimentalists have less of than they realize.

We also provide empirical leverage on the tricky question of how to appropriately operationalize the concepts we care about; empirical political scientists study "specific instances of units, treatments, observations, and settings" (Shadish, Cook, and Campbell, 2002), but figuring out the implications of those specifics can now more appropriately be guided by theory and empirics in combination.

Empirically, we test our theoretical framework through extensions of four well-known vignette-based survey experiments in political science along with three original experiments. Our extensions are based on Nicholson's (2012) exploration of elite cues, Press, Sagan, and Valentino's (2013) test of the nuclear taboo, Mutz and Kim's (2017) study of the role of in-group favoritism in trade preferences, and Tomz and Weeks' (2013) analysis of the democratic peace theory. Those are supplemented with three original experiments based on current events: protests related to racial justice and the Black Lives Matter movement, President Biden's selection of a vice-presidential running mate, and former President Trump's decision to withdraw from the World Health Organization. To each of these, we add our layers of experimental manipulations to test the implications of abstraction in experimental design. In the ELITE CUES experiment, we manipulate the actor identity of politicians presented in the vignette; for the IN-GROUP FAVORITISM study, we add two types of context ("filler" context and "charged" context likely to interact with the treatment), in the NUCLEAR WEAPONS experiment, we add manipulations on the levels of both context and actor identity, and in the DEMOCRATIC PEACE experiment, we vary the actor identities. In addition, for all of our experiments, we manipulate the degree of situational hypotheticality, presenting scenarios as either real, explicitly hypothetical, or in varying forms of ambiguous hypotheticality.

Our empirical results suggest reasons for optimism. How to frame the information provided in an experimental scenario presents an almost overwhelming menu of options for research, from describing the scenario as explicitly (or ambiguously) hypothetical, to saying that it is "real" (and thus potentially requiring the use of deception) or even setting the events in the future in order to avoid respondents anchoring too heavily on current events. And yet, we find that framing a study as hypothetical or real does not make a substantial difference in almost any of the studies.[43] This suggests that the difficult ethical decisions about whether or not to use deception may in many cases be avoided, adding empirical weight to an important normative debate in the field: our results suggest that framing vignettes as hypothetical generates substantively similar results compared to framing the same vignettes as "real" and avoids the use of deception.

We examined contextual detail in two ways: adding two types of context in the IN-GROUP FAVORITISM experiment to make it more rich and concrete, and subtracting context from the NUCLEAR WEAPONS experiment to render the scenario more abstract. Our results are consistent across both studies: in the vignette experiments we replicate here, we find that additional context leads to more conservative estimates of treatment effects. Investigating further, we find that the additional context dampens treatment effects by hindering respondents' ability to successfully recall the main treatment. Additionally, "charged" context has a greater dampening effect relative to "filler context," highlighting the importance of using theory and pilot studies to figure out what type of context is likely to interact with the experimental treatments and subject pools. Choosing the appropriate level of contextual detail in experimental work thus depends on how much statistical power the author expects, as well as the purpose of the study: if the purpose is to demonstrate that an effect exists, a sparser experimental design better enables researchers to identify this effect, but if the purpose is instead to understand how important an effect might be relative to other considerations, or whether respondents in a more naturalistic setting would be likely to receive the treatment (Barabas and Jerit, 2010), a more contextually rich design may be beneficial.

We also investigated the effects of varying the level of abstraction of the actors in the experiments. We manipulated actor identity in the NUCLEAR

---

[43] Only in the PROTEST experiment does presenting the scenario as occuring in the future (in the year 2030) have a modest moderating effect on the main treatment effect.

WEAPONS experiment by exposing respondents to conditions in which the country was either unnamed (baseline), fictional ("Malaguay"), or real and either consistent with the main thrust of the scenario – schema and treatment consistent ("Syria") – or schema inconsistent ("Bolivia"), the consistency having been ascertained via an earlier pilot experiment. Similarly, in the DEMOCRATIC PEACE experiments we manipulated actor identity by assigning respondents to conditions in which the country was either unnamed (baseline), fictional ("Malaguay") or a real country that was relatively treatment and schema consistent ("Turkey"), schema consistent and treatment inconsistent ("Iran"), or both treatment and schema inconsistent ("Ecuador"). In the ELITE CUES experiment, actor identity was manipulated using made-up, low-salience, or high-salience cue-givers.

Across these experiments, which considered different types of actors (i.e. countries or politicians), most actor-related design choices did not matter, in that the interaction between the actor identity treatment and the main treatment was not statistically significant. However, there are some types of actor identities that significantly shape experimental results. We find that using a treatment-inconsistent actor, such as Iran in the DEMOCRATIC PEACE experiments, undermines the main treatment effect, which appears to be driven by respondents either ignoring, or setting aside, the treatment when it is inconsistent with the actor used in the study (a phenomenon that is exacerbated among more knowledgeable respondents). Put simply: researchers must make sure that the actor identities they use are equally plausible across experimental conditions with problems arising to the extent that actors are described with features that contradict respondents' expectations or understanding. We also find that more salient politicians make more effective cuegivers than fictional cuegivers do.

In line with other recent work seeking to subject widely held assumptions about experimental methods to empirical scrutiny (Mullinix et al., 2015; Coppock, 2019; Mummolo and Peterson, 2019; Kertzer, 2020; Clifford, Sheagley, and Piston, 2021), we find that some design dimensions, such as situational hypotheticality, have almost no effect on experimental outcomes, whereas contextual detail and actor identities can significantly alter experimental findings. Our conceptual framework and empirical results clarify where, when, and how researchers have discretion in selecting particular levels of abstraction in their experimental stimuli.

References

Adida, Claire L. 2015. "Do African Voters Favor Coethnics? Evidence from a Survey Experiment in Benin." *Journal of Experimental Political Science* 2(1):1–11.

Aguinis, Herman, and Kyle J. Bradley. 2014. "Best Practice Recommendations for Designing and Implementing Experimental Vignette Methodology Studies." *Organizational Research Methods* 17(4):351–71.

Alekseev, Aleksandr, Gary Charness and Uri Gneezy. 2017. "Experimental Methods: When and Why Contextual Instructions Are Important." *Journal of Economic Behavior & Organization* 134:48–59.

Alexander, Cheryl S., and Henry Jay Becker. 1978. "The Use of Vignettes in Survey Research." *Public Opinion Quarterly* 42(1):93–104.

Althaus, Scott L. 1998. "Information Effects in Collective Preferences." *American Political Science Review* 92(3):545–58.

Arceneaux, Kevin. 2012. "Cognitive Biases and the Strength of Political Arguments." *American Journal of Political Science* 56(2):271–85.

Banerjee, Abhijit, Donald P. Green, Jeffery McManus and Rohini Pande. 2014. "Are Poor Voters Indifferent to Whether Elected Leaders are Criminal or Corrupt? A Vignette Experiment in Rural India." *Political Communication* 31(3):391–407.

Bansak, Kirk, Jens Hainmueller, Daniel J. Hopkins and Teppei Yamamoto. 2021. "Beyond the Breaking Point? Survey Satisficing in Conjoint Experiments." *Political Science Research and Methods* 9(1):53–71.

Barabas, Jason, and Jennifer Jerit. 2010. "Are Survey Experiments Externally Valid?" *American Political Science Review* 104(2):226–42.

Bassan-Nygate, Lotem, and Chagai M Weiss. 2022. "Party Competition and Cooperation Shape Affective Polarization: Evidence from Natural and Survey Experiments in Israel." *Comparative Political Studies* 55(2):287–318.

Baum, Matthew A., and Tim Groeling. 2009. "Shot by the Messenger: Partisan Cues and Public Opinion Regarding National Security and War." *Political Behavior* 31(2):157–86.

Bell, Mark S., and Kai Quek. 2018. "Authoritarian Public Opinion and the Democratic Peace." *International Organization* 72(1):227–42.

Berinsky, Adam J. 2009. *In Time of War: Understanding American Public Opinion from World War II to Iraq.* University of Chicago Press.

Berinsky, Adam J., Gregory A Huber and Gabriel S Lenz. 2012. "Evaluating Online Labor Markets for Experimental Research." *Political Analysis* 20(3):351–68.

Bertrand, Marianne, and Sendhil Mullainathan. 2004. "Are Emily and Greg More Employable Than Lakisha and Jamal? A Field Experiment on Labor Market Discrimination." *American Economic Review* 94(4):991–1013.

Boettcher, III, William A. 2004. "The Prospects for Prospect Theory: An Empirical Evaluation of International Relations Applications of Framing and Loss Aversion." *Political Psychology* 25(3):331–62.

Boettcher III, William A., and Michael D Cobb. 2006. "Echoes of Vietnam? Casualty Framing and Public Perceptions of Success and Failure in Iraq." *Journal of Conflict Resolution* 50(6):831–54.

Bostyn, Dries H., Sybren Sevenhant and Arne Roets. 2018. "Of Mice, Men, and Trolleys: Hypothetical Judgment versus Real-Life Behavior in Trolley-Style Moral Dilemmas." *Psychological Science* 29(7):1084–93.

Bracic, Ana, and Amanda Murdie. 2020. "Human Rights Abused? Terrorist Labeling and Individual Reactions to Call to Action." *Political Research Quarterly* 73(4):878–92.

Brader, Ted, Nicholas A. Valentino and Elizabeth Suhay. 2008. "What Triggers Public Opposition to Immigration? Anxiety, Group Cues, and Imigration." *American Journal of Political Science* 52(4):959–78.

Brooks, Deborah Jordan and Benjamin A. Valentino. 2011. "A War of One's Own: Understanding the Gender Gap in Support for War." *Public Opinion Quarterly* 75(2):270–86.

Brutger, Ryan. 2021. "The Power of Compromise: Proposal Power, Partisanship, and Public Support in International Bargaining." *World Politics* 73(1):128–66.

Brutger, Ryan, and Alexandra Guisinger. 2021. "Labor Market Volatility, Gender, and Trade Preferences." *Journal of Experimental Political Science*: 1–14. https://doi.org/10.1017/XPS.2021.9

Brutger, Ryan, and Brian Rathbun. 2021. "Fair Share?: Equality and Equity in American Attitudes towards Trade." *International Organization* 75(3):880–900.

Brutger, Ryan, and Anton Strezhnev. 2022. "International Investment Disputes, Media Coverage, and Backlash against International Law." *Journal of Conflict Resolution* 66(6):983–1009.

Brutger, Ryan, Joshua D. Kertzer, Jonathan Renshon, Dustin Tingley and Chagai M. Weiss. 2022. "Abstraction and Detail in Experimental Design." *American Journal of Political Science*. Early View. https://doi.org/10.1111/ajps.12710.

Burden, Barry C., and Casey A. Klofstad. 2005. "Affect and Cognition in Party Identification." *Political Psychology* 26(6):869–86.

Burge, Camille, Julian J. Wamble and Rachel Cuomo. 2020. "A Certain Type of Descriptive Representative? Understanding How the Skin Tone and Gender of Candidates Influences Black Politics." *Journal of Politics* 82(4):1596–601.

Bush, Sarah Sunn, and Pär Zetterberg. 2021. "Gender Quotas and International Reputation." *American Journal of Political Science* 65(2):326–41.

Butler, Daniel M., and David E. Broockman. 2011. "Do Politicians Racially Discriminate Against Constituents? A Field Experiment on State Legislators." *American Journal of Political Science* 55(3):436–77.

Butler, Daniel M., David W. Nickerson et al. 2011. "Can Learning Constituency Opinion Affect How Legislators Vote? Results from a Field Experiment." *Quarterly Journal of Political Science* 6(1):55–83.

Butler, Daniel M., and Eleanor Neff Powell. 2014. "Understanding the Party Brand: Experimental Evidence on the Role of Valence." *The Journal of Politics* 76(2):492–505.

Cacioppo, John T., and Richard E. Petty. 1982. "The Need for Cognition." *Journal of Personality and Social Psychology* 42(1):116–31.

Camerer, Colin. 1997. "Rules for Experimenting in Psychology and Economics, and Why They Differ." In *Understanding Strategic Interaction* ed. Wulf Albers, Werner Güth, Peter Hammerstein, Benny Moldovanu and Eric Damme. Springer: 313–27.

Cantor, Nancy, and Walter Mischel. 1979. "Prototypes in Person Perception." *Advances in Experimental Social Psychology* 12:3–52.

Chandler, Jesse, Pam Mueller and Gabriele Paolacci. 2014. "Nonnaivete among Amazon Mechanical Turk Workers: Consequences and Solutions for Behavioral Researchers." *Behavioral Research Methods* 46(1):112–30.

Chapman, Terrence L., and Stephen Chaudoin. 2020. "Public Reactions to International Legal Institutions: The International Criminal Court in a Developing Democracy." *The Journal of Politics* 82(4):1305–20.

Chong, Dennis, and James N. Druckman. 2007. "Framing Public Opinion in Competitive Democracies." *American Political Science Review* 101(4):637–55.

Clarke, Kevin A., and David M. Primo. 2012. *A Model Discipline: Political Science and the Logic of Representations*. Oxford University Press.

Clary, Christopher, and Niloufer Siddiqui. 2021. "Voters and Foreign Policy: Evidence from a Conjoint Experiment in Pakistan." *Foreign Policy Analysis* 17(2):1–13.

Clifford, Scott, Geoffrey Sheagley and Spencer Piston. 2021. "Increasing Precision without Altering Treatment Effects: Repeated Measures Designs in Survey Experiments." *American Political Science Review* 115(3):1048–65.

Colburn, Timothy, and Gary Shute. 2007. "Abstraction in Computer Science." *Minds and Machines* 17(2):169–84.

Colleau, Sophie M., Kevin Glynn, Steven Lybrand et al. 1990. "Symbolic Racism in Candidate Evaluation: An Experiment." *Political Behavior* 12(4):385–402.

Collier, David, and Robert Adcock. 2001. "Measurement Validity: A Shared Standard for Qualitative and Quantitative Research." *American Political Science Review* 95(3):529–46.

Converse, Jean M., and Stanley Presser. 1986. *Survey Questions: Handcrafting the Standardized Questionnaire*. SAGE Publications.

Coppock, Alexander. 2019. "Generalizing from Survey Experiments Conducted on Mechanical Turk: A Replication Approach." *Political Science Research and Methods* 7(3):613–28.

Coppock, Alexander, and Oliver A. McClellan. 2019. "Validating the Demographic, Political, Psychological, and Experimental Results Obtained from a New Source of Online Survey Respondents." *Research & Politics* 6(1):2053168018822174.

Croco, Sarah E., Michael J. Hanmer and Jared A. McDonald. 2021. "At What Cost? Reexamining Audience Costs in Realistic Settings." *Journal of Politics* 83(1). https://doi.org/10.1086/708912.

Dafoe, Allan, Baobao Zhang and Devin Caughey. 2018. "Information Equivalence in Survey Experiments." *Political Analysis* 26(4):399–416.

Dawes, Christopher T., Peter John Loewen and James H. Fowler. 2011. "Social Preferences and Political Participation." *The Journal of Politics* 73(3):845–56.

Delli Carpini, Michael X., and Scott Keeter. 1996. *What Americans Know about Politics and Why It Matters*. Yale University Press.

Dickson, Eric S. 2009. "Do Participants and Observers Assess Intentions Differently During Bargaining and Conflict?" *American Journal of Political Science* 53(4):910–30.

Dickson, Eric S. 2011. "Economics vs. Psychology Experiments: Stylization, Incentives, and Deception." In *Handbook of Experimental Political Science*, ed. James N. Druckman, Donald P. Green, James H. Kuklinski and Arthur Lupia. Cambridge University Press.

Dill, Janina, and Livia I. Schubiger. 2021. "Attitudes toward the Use of Force: Instrumental Imperatives, Moral Principles, and International Law." *American Journal of Political Science* 65(3):612–33.

Druckman, James N. 2003. "The Power of Television Images: The First Kennedy-Nixon Debate Revisited." *Journal of Politics* 65(2):559–71.

Druckman, James N., and Kjersten R. Nelson. 2003. "Framing and Deliberation: How Citizens' Conversations Limit Elite Influence." *American Journal of Political Science* 47(4):729–45.

Druckman, James N., and Cindy D. Kam. 2011. "Students as Experimental Participants: A Defense of the 'Narrow Data Base'." In *Handbook of Experimental Political Science*, ed. James N. Druckman, Donald P. Green, James H. Kuklinski and Arthur Lupia. Cambridge University Press: 41–57.

Druckman, James N., Erik Peterson and Rune Slothuus. 2013. "How Elite Partisan Polarization Affects Public Opinion Formation." *American Political Science Review* 107(1):57–79.

Dunning, Thad, and Lauren Harrison. 2010. "Cross-cutting Cleavages and Ethnic Voting: An Experimental Study of Cousinage in Mali." *American Political Science Review* 104(1):21–39.

Edwards, Pearce, and Daniel Arnon. 2021. "Violence on Many Sides: Framing Effects on Protest and Support for Repression." *British Journal of Political Science* 51(2):488–506.

Evers, Miles M., Aleksandr Fisher and Steven D. Schaaf. 2019. "Is There a Trump Effect? An Experiment on Political Polarization and Audience Costs." *Perspectives on Politics* 17(2):433–52.

FeldmanHall, Oriel, Dean Mobbs, Davy Evans, et al. 2012. "What We Say and What We Do: The Relationship between Real and Hypothetical Moral Choices." *Cognition* 123(3):434–41.

Findley, Michael G., Daniel L. Nielson and J. C. Sharman. 2013. "Using Field Experiments in International Relations: A Randomized Study of Anonymous Incorporation." *International Organization* 67(4):657–93.

Findley, Michael G., Kyosuke Kikuta and Michael Denly. 2021. "External Validity." *Annual Review of Political Science* 24:365–93.

Fiske, Susan T., Richard R. Lau and Richard A. Smith. 1990. "On the Varieties and Utilities of Political Expertise." *Social Cognition* 8(1):31–48.

Friedman, Sunder, Daniel Friedman and Shyam Sunder. 1994. *Experimental Methods: A Primer for Economists*. Cambridge University Press.

Gadarian, Shana Kushner, Sara Wallace Goodman and Thomas Pepinsky. 2021. "Partisan Endorsement Experiments Do Not Affect Mass Opinion on COVID-19." *Journal of Elections, Public Opinion and Parties* 31 (S1):122–31.

Gaddis, S. Michael. 2017. "How Black are Lakisha and Jamal? Racial Perceptions from Names Used in Correspondence Audit Studies." *Sociological Science* 4:469–89.

Gaines, Brian J., James H. Kuklinski and Paul J. Quirk. 2007. "The Logic of the Survey Experiment Reexamined." *Political Analysis* 15(1):1–20.

Green-Riley, Naima, Dominika Kruszewska-Eduardo and Ze Fu. 2021. "Teargas and Selfie Cams: Foreign Protests and Media in the Digital Age." *Journal of Experimental Political Science*. First View. 1–13. https://doi.org/10.1017/XPS.2021.1

Guisinger, Alexandra. 2017. *American Opinion on Trade: Preferences without Politics*. Oxford University Press.

Haas, Nicholas, and Rebecca B Morton. 2018. "Saying versus Doing: A New Donation Method for Measuring Ideal Points." *Public Choice* 176(1):79–106.

Habyarimana, James, Macartan Humphreys, Daniel N. Posner and Jeremy M. Weinstein. 2007. "Why Does Ethnic Diversity Undermine Public Goods Provision?" *American Political Science Review* 101(4):709–25.

Hainmueller, Jens, and Daniel J. Hopkins. 2015. "The Hidden American Immigration Consensus: A Conjoint Analysis of Attitudes toward Immigrants." *American Journal of Political Science* 59(3):529–48.

Hainmueller, Jens, Dominik Hangartner and Teppei Yamamoto. 2015. "Validating Vignette and Conjoint Survey Experiments against Real-World Behavior." *Proceedings of the National Academy of Sciences* 112(8):2395–400.

Hashtroudi, Shahin, Sharon A. Mutter, Elizabeth A. Cole and Susan K. Green. 1984. "Schema-Consistent and Schema-Inconsistent Information: Processing Demands." *Personality and Social Psychology Bulletin* 10(2):269–78.

Hastie, Reid, and Bernadette Park. 1986. "The Relationship between Memory and Judgment Depends on Whether the Judgment Task is Memory-Based or On-line." *Psychological review* 93(3):258.

Herrmann, Richard K. 2013. "Perceptions and Image Theory in International Relations." In *Oxford Handbook of Political Psychology*, ed. Leonie Huddy, David O. Sears and Jack S. Levy. 2nd ed. Oxford University Press: 334–63.

Herrmann, Richard K., Philip E. Tetlock and Penny S. Visser. 1999. "Mass Public Decisions on Go to War: A Cognitive-Interactionist Framework." *American Political Science Review* 93(3):553–73.

Hertwig, Ralph, and Andreas Ortmann. 2008. "Deception in Experiments: Revisiting the Arguments in Its Defense." *Ethics & behavior* 18(1):59–92.

Holland, Paul. 1986. "Statistics and Causal Inference." *Journal of the American Statistical Association* 81(395):945–60.

Horowitz, Michael C., and Matthew S. Levendusky. 2011. "Drafting Support for War: Conscription and Mass Support for Warfare." *Journal of Politics* 73(2):524–34.

Hsiao, Yuan, and Scott Radnitz. 2021. "Allies or Agitators? How Partisan Identity Shapes Public Opinion about Violent or Nonviolent Protests." *Political Communication* 38(4):479–97.

Huddleston, R. Joseph. 2019. "Think Ahead: Cost Discounting and External Validity in Foreign Policy Survey Experiments." *Journal of Experimental Political Science* 6(2):108–19.

Huddy, Leonie, and Nayda Terkildsen. 1993. "Gender Stereotypes and the Perception of Male and Female Candidates." *American Journal of Political Science* 37(1):119–47.

Huff, Connor, and Dominika Kruszewska. 2016. "Banners, Barricades, and Bombs: The Tactical Choices of Social Movements and Public Opinion." *Comparative Political Studies* 49(13):1774–808.

Huff, Connor, and Dustin Tingley. 2015. ""Who Are These People?" Evaluating the Demographic Characteristics and Political Preferences of MTurk Survey Respondents." *Research & Politics* 2(3). https://doi.org/10.1177/2053168015604648.

Hundley, Lindsay. 2020. "The Shadow of the Future and Bargaining Delay: An Experimental Approach." *Journal of Politics* 82(1):378–83.

Irwin, Julie R., Gary H. McClelland and William D. Schulze. 1992. "Hypothetical and Real Consequences in Experimental Auctions for Insurance against Low-Probability Risks." *Journal of Behavioral Decision Making* 5(2):107–16.

Johns, Robert, and Graeme A. M. Davies. 2012. "Democratic Peace or Clash of Civilizations? Target States and Support for War in Britain and the United States." *Journal of Politics* 74(4):1038–52.

Kam, Cindy D., and Elizabeth J. Zechmeister. 2013. "Name Recognition and Candidate Support." *American Journal of Political Science* 57(4):971–86.

Kanthak, Kristin, and Jonathan Woon. 2015. "Women Don't Run? Election Aversion and Candidate Entry." *American Journal of Political Science* 59(3):595–612.

Kertzer, Joshua D. 2017. "Microfoundations in International Relations." *Conflict Management and Peace Science* 34(1):81–97.

Kertzer, Joshua D. 2020. "Re-assessing Elite–Public Gaps in Political Behavior." *American Journal of Political Science*. Early View. https://doi.org/10.1111/ajps.12583.

Kertzer, Joshua D., and Brian C. Rathbun. 2015. "Fair Is Fair: Social Preferences and Reciprocity in International Politics." *World Politics* 67(4):613–55.

Kertzer, Joshua D., and Ryan Brutger. 2016. "Decomposing Audience Costs: Bringing the Audience Back into Audience Cost Theory." *American Journal of Political Science* 60(1):234–49.

Kertzer, Joshua D., and Thomas Zeitzoff. 2017. "A Bottom-Up Theory of Public Opinion about Foreign Policy." *American Journal of Political Science* 61(3):543–58.

Kertzer, Joshua D., Jonathan Renshon and Keren Yarhi-Milo. 2021. "How Do Observers Assess Resolve?" *British Journal of Political Science* 51(1):308–30.

Kertzer, Joshua D., Stephen G. Brooks and Deborah Jordan Brooks. 2021. "Do Partisan Types Stop at the Water's Edge?" *Journal of Politics* 83 (4):1764–82.

Kertzer, Joshua D., and Jonathan Renshon. 2022. "Elite Experiments and Surveys." *Annual Review of Political Science* 25: 529–50.

Klar, Samara. 2018. "When Common Identities Decrease Trust: An Experimental Study of Partisan Women." *American Journal of Political Science* 62(3):610–22.

Kreps, Sarah, and Stephen Roblin. 2019. "Treatment Format and External Validity in International Relations Experiments." *International Interactions* 45(3):576–94.

Kriner, Douglas L., and Francis X. Shen. 2014. "Reassessing American Casualty Sensitivity: The Mediating Influence of Inequality." *Journal of Conflict Resolution* 58(7):1174–201.

Landau-Wells, Marika. 2018. "Dealing with Danger: Threat Perception and Policy Preferences." Doctoral Dissertation, Massachusetts Institute of Technology.

Landgrave, Michelangelo, and Nicholas Weller. 2022. "Do Name-Based Treatments Violate Information Equivalence? Evidence from a Correspondence Audit Experiment." *Political Analysis* 30(1):142–48.

Lau, Richard R., Lee Sigelman and Ivy Brown Rovner. 2007. "The Effects of Negative Political Campaigns: A Meta-analytic Reassessment." *Journal of Politics* 69(4):1176–209.

Lenzner, Timo, Lars Kaczmirek and Alwine Lenzner. 2010. "Cognitive Burden of Survey Questions and Response Times: A Psycholinguistic Experiment." *Applied Cognitive Psychology* 24(7):1003–20.

LeVeck, Brad L., D. Alex Hughes, James H. Fowler, Emilie M. Hafner-Burton and David G. Victor. 2014. "The Role of Self-Interest in Elite Bargaining." *Proceedings of the National Academy of Sciences* 111(52):18536–41.

LeVeck, Brad L., and Neil Narang. 2017. "The Democratic Peace and the Wisdom of Crowds." *International Studies Quarterly* 61(4):867–80.

Levine, David K., and Thomas R. Palfrey. 2007. "The Paradox of Voter Participation? A Laboratory Study." *American Political Science Review* 101(1):143–58.

Lupton, Danielle L. 2019. "The External Validity of College Student Subject Pools in Experimental Research: A Cross-Sample Comparison of Treatment Effect Heterogeneity." *Political Analysis* 27(1):90–97.

Lyall, Jason, Graeme Blair and Kosuke Imai. 2013. "Explaining Support for Combatants during Wartime: A Survey Experiment in Afghanistan." *American Political Science Review* 107(4):679–705.

Lyall, Jason, Yang-Yang Zhou and Kosuke Imai. 2020. "Can Economic Assistance Shape Combatant Support in Wartime? Experimental Evidence from Afghanistan." *American Political Science Review* 114 (1):126–43.

Mason, Lilliana. 2018. *Uncivil Agreement: How Politics Became Our Identity*. University of Chicago Press.

Matanock, Aila M., and Natalia Garbiras-Díaz. 2018. "Considering Concessions: A Survey Experiment on the Colombian Peace Process." *Conflict Management and Peace Science* 35(6):637–55.

Matland, Richard E., and Güneş Murat Tezcür. 2011. "Women as Candidates: An Experimental Study in Turkey." *Politics & Gender* 7(3):365–90.

Mattes, Michaela, and Jessica L. P. Weeks. 2019. "Hawks, Doves and Peace: An Experimental Approach." *American Journal of Political Science* 63(1):53–66.

McDermott, Rose, and Jonathan Cowden. 2001. "The Effects of Uncertainty and Sex in a Crisis Simulation Game." *International Interactions* 27(4):353–80.

McDermott, Rose. 2002. "Experimental Methods in Political Science." *Annual Review of Political Science* 5:31–61.

McDermott, Rose, Dominic Johnson, Jonathan Cowden and Stephen Rosen. 2007. "Testosterone and Aggression in a Simulated Crisis Game." *Annals of the American Academy of Political and Social Science* 614 (1):15–33.

McDonald, Jared. 2020. "Avoiding the Hypothetical: Why 'Mirror Experiments' are an Essential Part of Survey Research." *International Journal of Public Opinion Research* 32(2):266–83.

McDonald, Jared, Sarah E. Croco and Candace Turitto. 2019. "Teflon Don or Politics as Usual? An Examination of Foreign Policy Flip-Flops in the Age of Trump." *Journal of Politics* 81(2):757–66.

Mendelberg, Tali. 2001. *The Race Card: Campaign Strategy, Implicit Messages, and the Norm of Equality*. Princeton University Press.

Mintz, Alex, and Nehemia Geva. 1993. "Why Don't Democracies Fight Each Other?: An Experimental Study." *Journal of Conflict Resolution* 37(3):484–503.

Morton, Rebecca B., and Kenneth C Williams. 2010. *Experimental Political Science and the Study of Causality: From Nature to the Lab*. Cambridge University Press.

Mullinix, Kevin J., Thomas J. Leeper, James N. Druckman and Jeremy Freese. 2015. "The Generalizability of Survey Experiments." *Journal of Experimental Political Science* 2(2):109–38.

Mummolo, Jonathan, and Erik Peterson. 2019. "Demand Effects in Survey Experiments: An Empirical Assessment." *American Political Science Review* 113(2):517–29.

Mutz, Diana C. 2011. *Population-Based Survey Experiments*. Princeton University Press.

Mutz, Diana C. 2021. "Improving Experimental Treatments in Political Science." In *Advances in Experimental Political Science*, ed. James N. Druckman and Donald P. Green. Cambridge University Press: 219–38.

Mutz, Diana C., and Eunji Kim. 2017. "The Impact of In-Group Favoritism on Trade Preferences." *International Organization* 71 (4) :827–50.

Nelson, Thomas E., Rosalee A. Clawson and Zoe M. Oxley. 1997. "Media Framing of a Civil Liberties Conflict and Its Effect on Tolerance." *American Political Science Review* 91(3):567–83.

Nicholson, Stephen P. 2012. "Polarizing Cues." *American Journal of Political Science* 56(1):52–66.

Nielson, Daniel L., Susan D. Hyde and Judith Kelley. 2019. "The Elusive Sources of Legitimacy Beliefs: Civil Society Views of International Election Observers." *The Review of International Organizations* 14 (4):685–715.

Paivio, Allan. 1990. *Mental Representations: A Dual Coding Approach*. Oxford University Press.

Petsko, Christopher D., and Galen V. Bodenhausen. 2019. "Racial Stereotyping of Gay Men: Can a Minority Sexual Orientation Erase Race?" *Journal of Experimental Social Psychology* 83:37–54.

Porter, Ethan, and Yamil R. Velez. 2022. "Placebo Selection in Survey Experiments: An Agnostic Approach." *Political Analysis* First View:1–14. https://doi.org/10.1017/pan.2021.16.

Press, Daryl G., Scott D. Sagan and Benjamin A. Valentino. 2013. "Atomic Aversion: Experimental Evidence on Taboos, Traditions, and the Non-use of Nuclear Weapons." *American Political Science Review* 107 (1): 188–206.

Quek, Kai. 2017. "Rationalist Experiments on War." *Political Science Research and Methods* 5(1):123–42.

Raffler, P.J., 2020. Does political oversight of the bureaucracy increase accountability? Field experimental evidence from a dominant party regime. *American Political Science Review*. Early View. https://doi.org/10.1017/S0003055422000181

Rathbun, Brian C., Joshua D. Kertzer and Mark Paradis. 2017. "Homo diplomaticus: Mixed-Method Evidence of Variation in Strategic Rationality 71:S1." *International Organization*: S33–S60.

Reeves, Andrew, and Jon C. Rogowski. 2018. "The Public Cost of Unilateral Action." *American Journal of Political Science* 62(2):424–40.

Reiley, David. 2015. "The Lab and the Field: Empirical and Experimental Economics." In *Handbook of Experimental Economic Methodology*, ed. Guillaume R. Fréchette and Andrew Schotter. Oxford University Press: 410–12.

Renshon, Jonathan. 2015. "Losing Face and Sinking Costs: Experimental Evidence on the Judgment of Political and Military Leaders." *International Organization* 69(3):659–95.

Renshon, Jonathan, Allan Dafoe and Paul Huth. 2018. "Leader Influence and Reputation Formation in World Politics." *American Journal of Political Science* 62(2):325–39.

Rosenwasser, Shirley M., Robyn R. Rogers, Sheila Fling, Kayla Silvers-Pickens and John Butemeyer. 1987. "Attitudes toward Women and Men in Politics: Perceived Male and Female Candidate Competencies and Participant Personality Characteristics." *Political Psychology* 8(2): 191–200.

Rousseau, David L., and Rocio Garcia-Retamero. 2007. "Identity, Power, and Threat Perception: A Cross-national Experimental Study." *Journal of Conflict Resolution* 51(5):744–71.

Rousu, Matthew C., Gregory Colson, Jay R. Corrigan, Carola Grebitus and Maria L. Loureiro. 2015. "Deception in Experiments: Towards Guidelines on Use in Applied Economics Research." *Applied Economic Perspectives and Policy* 37(3):524–36.

Rubenzer, Trevor, and Steven B. Redd. 2010. "Ethnic Minority Groups and US Foreign Policy: Examining Congressional Decision Making and Economic Sanctions." *International Studies Quarterly* 54(3):755–77.

Sanbonmatsu, Kira. 2002. "Gender Stereotypes and Vote Choice." *American Journal of Political Science* 46(1):20–34.

Sartori, Giovanni. 1970. "Concept Misformation in Comparative Politics." *American Political Science Review* 64(4):1033–53.

Saunders, Elizabeth N. 2018. "Leaders, Advisers, and the Political Origins of Elite Support for War." *Journal of Conflict Resolution* 62(10):2118–49.

Schneider, Monica C. 2014. "The Effects of Gender-Bending on Candidate Evaluations." *Journal of Women, Politics & Policy* 35(1):55–77.

Semin, Gün R., and Klaus Fiedler. 1988. "The Cognitive Functions of Linguistic Categories in Describing Persons: Social Cognition and Language." *Journal of Personality and Social Psychology* 54(4):558–68.

Shadish, William, Thomas D. Cook and Donald Thomas Campbell. 2002. *Experimental and Quasi-experimental Designs for Generalized Causal Inference*. Houghton Mifflin.

Shapira, Oren, Nira Liberman, Yaacov Trope and SoYon Rim. 2012. "Levels of Mental Construal." In *SAGE Handbook of Social Cognition*, ed. Susan T. Fiske and C. Neil Macrae. SAGE Publications: 229–50.

Smith, Vernon L. 1976. "Experimental Economics: Induced Value Theory." *The American Economic Review* 66(2):274–79.

Sniderman, Paul M. 2011. "The Logic and Design of the Survey Experiment: An Autobiography of a Methodological Innovation." In *Handbook of Experimental Political Science*, ed. James N. Druckman, Donald P. Green, James H. Kuklinski and Arthur Lupia. Cambridge University Press: 102–14.

Steiner, Peter M., Christiane Atzmüller and Dan Su. 2016. "Designing Valid and Reliable Vignette Experiments for Survey Research: A Case Study on the Fair Gender Income Gap." *Journal of Methods and Measurement in the Social Sciences* 7(2):52–94.

Tankard, Margaret E., and Elizabeth Levy Paluck. 2017. "The Effect of a Supreme Court Decision Regarding Gay Marriage on Social Norms and Personal Attitudes." *Psychological Science* 28(9):1334–44.

Tannenwald, Nina. 1999. "The Nuclear Taboo: The United States and the Normative Basis of Nuclear Non-Use." *International Organization* 53(3):433–68.

Teele, Dawn Langan, Joshua Kalla and Frances Rosenbluth. 2018. "The Ties That Double Bind: Social Roles and Women's Underrepresentation in Politics." *American Political Science Review* 112(3):525–41.

Tingley, Dustin. 2017. "Rising Power on the Mind." *International Organization* 71(S1):S165–S188.

Tingley, Dustin, and Barbara Walter. 2011a. "Reputation Building in International Relations: An Experimental Approach." *International Organization* 65(2):343–65.

Tingley, Dustin, and Barbara Walter. 2011b. "The Effect of Repeated Play on Reputation Building: An Experimental Approach." *International Organization* 65(2):343–65.

Tomz, Michael. 2007. "Domestic Audience Costs in International Relations: An Experimental Approach." *International Organization* 61(4):821–40.

Tomz, Michael, and Jessica Weeks. 2013. "Public Opinion and the Democratic Peace." *American Political Science Review* 107(4):849–65.

Tomz, Michael, Jessica Weeks and Keren Yarhi-Milo. 2020. "Public Opinion and Decisions about Military Force in Democracies." *International Organization* 74(1):119–43.

Trager, Robert F., and Lynn Vavreck. 2011. "The Political Costs of Crisis Bargaining: Presidential Rhetoric and the Role of Party." *American Journal of Political Science* 55(3):526–45.

Trope, Yaacov, and Nira Liberman. 2003. "Temporal Construal." *Psychological Review* 110(3):403–21.

Trope, Yaacov, and Nira Liberman. 2010. "Construal-Level Theory of Psychological Distance." *Psychological Review* 117(2):440–63.

Valentino, Nicholas A., Fabian G. Neuner and L. Matthew Vandenbroek. 2018. "The Changing Norms of Racial Political Rhetoric and the End of Racial Priming." *The Journal of Politics* 80(3):757–71.

von Borzyskowski, Inken, and Felicity Vabulas. 2021. "When Is It 'OK' to Leave?: U.S. Public Opinion toward Withdrawal from International Organizations." Working paper.

Wamble, Julian J. 2020. "The Chosen One: How Community Commitment makes Certain Representatives More Preferable." Working paper. https://www.julianwamble.com/_files/ugd/947e22_6a70c4f1b6c248a28020fdca4ded73d8.pdf.

White, Ariel, Anton Strezhnev, Christopher Lucas, Dominika Kruszewska and Connor Huff. 2018. "Investigator Characteristics and Respondent Behavior in Online Surveys." *Journal of Experimental Political Science* 5(1):56–67.

White, Ariel R., Noah L. Nathan and Julie K. Faller. 2015. "What Do I Need to Vote? Bureaucratic Discretion and Discrimination by Local Election Officials." *American Political Science Review* 109(1):129–42.

Xu, Sihua, Yu Pan, Zhe Qu et al. 2018. "Differential Effects of Real versus Hypothetical Monetary Reward Magnitude on Risk-Taking Behavior and Brain Activity." *Scientific Reports* 8(1):1–9.

Yanow, Dvora, and Peregrine Schwartz-Shea. 2016. "Encountering Your IRB 2.0: What Political Scientists Need to Know." *PS: Political Science & Politics* 49(2):277–86.

Yarhi-Milo, Keren, Joshua D. Kertzer and Jonathan Renshon. 2018. "Tying Hands, Sinking Costs, and Leader Attributes." *Journal of Conflict Resolution* 62(10):2150–79.

Acknowledgments

The project this Element is based on was initially conceived in late-night conversations at the La Jolla Shores Hotel restaurant bar at University of California–San Diego in the winter of 2014. We're grateful to Marc Paradis for his insights in those early conversations, as well as to Dustin Tingley, with whom we published an article on the topic in the *American Journal of Political Science*, portions of which are included in this manuscript. We are grateful to the editors of the *American Journal of Political Science* for their support and for letting us build from the material from our article in this Element. For detailed and helpful comments, we're particularly appreciative of Jamie Druckman, as well as Adam Berinsky, Soubhik Barari, Adam Seth Levine, Jonathan Mummolo, Rich Nielsen, Anne Sartori, Jonathan Woon, and Teppei Yamamoto. The project also benefited immensely from feedback provided by audiences at the MIT's Political Experiments Research Lab in 2014, the Midwest Political Science Association conference in 2019, the American Political Science Association conference in 2020, and the New York University Experiments Conference in 2020, along with some very spirited comments from anonymous reviewers. Ryan is extremely grateful for Alex, Bryson, and Sage for their support and patience while working on this project. Josh thanks Nick for everything, and can't think of anyone else with whom he'd rather be trapped in a global pandemic. Jonathan was lucky to be the beneficiary of Michelle's patience, support, and wisdom over the course of this project. Mira did more than her part by distracting her dad when he needed it. Chagai thanks Aba and Ima for endless support and encouragement from close and afar, and Naomi for all the moments of happiness and laughter.

Cambridge Elements ☰

Experimental Political Science

James N. Druckman
Northwestern University

James N. Druckman is the Payson S. Wild Professor of Political Science and the Associate Director of the Institute for Policy Research at Northwestern University. He served as an editor for the journals Political Psychology and Public Opinion Quarterly as well as the University of Chicago Press's series in American Politics. He currently is the co-Principal Investigator of Time-Sharing Experiments for the Social Sciences (TESS) and sits on the American National Election Studies' Board. He previously served as President of the American Political Science Association section on Experimental Research and helped oversee the launching of the Journal of Experimental Political Science. He was co-editor of the Cambridge Handbook of Experimental Political Science. He is a Fellow of the American Academy of Arts and Sciences and has published more than 100 articles/book chapters on public opinion, political communication, campaigns, research methods, and other topics.

About the Series
There currently are few outlets for extended works on experimental methodology in political science. The new Experimental Political Science Cambridge Elements series features research on experimental approaches to a given substantive topic, and experimental methods by prominent and upcoming experts in the field.

Cambridge Elements ≡

Experimental Political Science

Elements in the Series

A full series listing is available at: www.cambridge.org/QCMSS

Printed in the United States
by Baker & Taylor Publisher Services